D1460624

An Incredible Journey

From the house of bondage to the promised land

By: Samuel T. Carson

By the same author:
The Genesis Brides,
The Long Road Home,
Songs of the Servant King
and other works.

An Incredible Journey traces the story of the children
of Israel, from the time of their slavery in Egypt, until
they entered their promised land, the land of Canaan.
It highlights many remarkable and unmistakable
parallels between their pilgrimage and our own, and it
shows that their environment has more in common
with ours than perhaps we ever imagined. This book is
very relevant to Christians living in the twenty-first
century.

AN INCREDIBLE JOURNEY
© 2002 Samuel T. Carson

ISBN   1 84030 123 6

Ambassador Publications
a·division of
Ambassador Productions Ltd.
Providence House
Ardenlee Street
Belfast BT6 8QJ
Northern Ireland
www.ambassador-productions.com

Emerald House
427 Wade Hampton Blvd
Greenville
SC 29609
USA
www.emeraldhouse.com

CONTENTS

Introduction
Heaven's object lesson

STAGE ONE
The Redeemed of the Lord
(From Rameses to the Red Sea)

STAGE TWO
The Life of Faith
(From the Red Sea to Sinai)

STAGE THREE
The Spiritual and the Carnal mind
(From Sinai to Kadesh Barnea)

STAGE FOUR
The Years of Wandering
(From Kadesh, and then back to Kadesh)

Stage Four (Contd.)
An Interlude
(In the plains of Moab and at Baal-peor)

STAGE FIVE
Home at last
(From the plains of Moab to the Promised Land)

SUBJECT INDEX

Introduction

Heaven's Object Lesson

Found mainly in the first five books of the Bible, the writings of Moses present us with an incredible object lesson. The lesson is in five parts and forms a marvellously comprehensive picture gallery. It brims with what have been aptly termed heaven-drawn pictures. These pictures illustrate practically all the salient truths of the New Testament revelation.

Since this great object lesson is presented in pictorial form, it enables us to grasp more easily the various facets of any given truth. Although we are dealing only with the first part of it in this volume, the five parts in the object lesson may be listed as follows:

1. The Journey from Egypt to Canaan
2. The Tabernacle
3. The Priesthood
4. The Offerings
5. The Feasts

It was of these very things Paul declared, "whatsoever things were written aforetime were written for our learning, that we, through patience and comfort of the scriptures, might have hope" (Rom.15:4). We must confess to our shame that these things have become as a closed book today. The Christian Church at the beginning of the twenty first century is woefully ignorant of these refreshing springs of spiritual wisdom.

This lack of attention to the types and shadows of the Old Testament has resulted in much confusion, and not a little division, in the fellowships of God's people. Moreover, it is to be feared that the neglect of these things has had a debilitating effect on the Christian testimony as a whole, and has even led, we believe, to a lowering in the general tone of spiritual experience.

Our intention in An Incredible Journey is to look at the children of Israel, from the time of their slavery in the house of bondage in Egypt, until they entered their promised land, the land of Canaan. In doing so we will keep in mind that we too are engaged in a journey. As we follow their course, we will notice many quite unmistakable parallels between their pilgrimage and our own. And we will discover that their environment, in that waste and barren wilderness, has much more in common with ours than perhaps we imagined.

We will not stop at their every encampment, but we will take an overview of the journey itself and highlight some of its more prominent features. In this exercise it will be convenient and helpful for us to bear in mind that the total journey may also be divided into five clearly identifiable stages. A summary of these five divisions would be as follows,

1. From Rameses in Egypt, to the Red Sea
2. From the Red Sea to Sinai
3. From the wilderness of Sinai, to Paran
4. From the wilderness of Paran to Baal-peor
5. From Baal-peor to the Jordan river and the land

The philosophy behind Israel's journey is of universal application. The basic lesson was this: "That man does not live by bread alone, but by every word that proceeds out of the mouth of God" (Deut.8:3). It is a difficult lesson to learn and it is taught in a hard school, like the one Israel passed through in the great wilderness.

Stage One
The Redeemed of the Lord
(From Rameses to the Red Sea)

Chapter 1
In the House of Bondage

And the Lord said ... I know their sorrows.
Exodus. 3:7.

The book of Exodus begins with Abraham's descendants in dire
servitude in the land of Egypt. Under the domination of Pharaoh
the king, they had to endure the tyranny of his cruel taskmasters.
They were not just a subject people, they were slaves suffering a
harsh oppression. They had no strength, and left to themselves in
their servile state, they had no hope of deliverance.

In the spiritual realm, believers today will see striking parallels
between themselves in their unregenerate state, and the unhappy
story of Israel's Egyptian slavery. Sold under sin is how the New
Testament summarises our case. (See Rom.7:14.) True, this is the
language of the slave market, but as the drama of Israel's mighty
deliverance unfolds, we shall see that the language is entirely apt.

The Times of Joseph

The book of Genesis gives us the family history of these people
who now found themselves in the house of bondage, while the
book of Exodus marks the beginning of their national history. The
fascinating account of how the children of Israel came to be in this
sorry predicament in the first place is recorded in considerable
detail as part of the story of Joseph. (See Gen.46 & 47.)

There was a great famine in those days and Joseph's brothers, who
had earlier betrayed him and sold him into servitude, were
compelled to come and buy corn at the renowned granaries he had
established throughout Egypt. Just before this, Joseph had become

Lord over all the land, but his brothers were totally unaware of his exalted position.

When they first came down to Egypt they did not realize who it was they were dealing with, although Joseph recognized them. But with characteristic prudence, he did not immediately make himself known to the brothers. There had to be a time of probing and proving first. Even so, when it came, the reunion was not an easy one. It took place in an atmosphere charged with deep emotion.

Joseph began by enquiring about Jacob, his father. In their case a quite special bond existed between father and son. The token of this bond was the famous coat of many colours. When Joseph learned that his father still survived, he sent chariots and an abundance of provision, to bring him and the entire family down to Egypt.

Joseph is yet alive

When the brothers returned home and burst in upon Jacob with the startling news that Joseph was yet alive, it was all too much for the aged patriarch. He was convinced that Joseph had long since died. Some wild beast had surely devoured him. But when he heard Joseph's words of gracious entreaty, and when he saw the provision Joseph had sent to carry him down to Egypt, he was finally persuaded. He said, "It is enough: Joseph my son is yet alive; I will go and see him before I die" (Gen. 45:28).

In all these things it is not difficult to see in Joseph a splendid type of Christ. Joseph was beloved by his father, and he was hated by his brethren, who betrayed him, and sold him into the hands of the Gentiles. Going down into Egypt, and going down further into prison, he pictures the Lord Jesus going down into death. And our Saviour's resurrection is surely before us in the message that his sons brought to back Jacob, they said, Joseph is yet alive.

Before taking his journey to Egypt, Jacob, who was now called Israel, sought the guidance of God. He went to Beer-sheba where he sacrificed to the Lord. It was there in a night vision that the Lord appeared to him and said, "Fear not to go down into Egypt; for I will there make of you a great nation" (Gen.46:3). At that time Israel was also given several important assurances about the future. "I will go down with you into Egypt; and I will also surely bring you up again; and Joseph shall put his hand upon your eyes" (Gen.46:4).

Jacob goes down to Egypt

Having received such promises from the Lord, Israel was reassured, and so he set out on the long journey to Egypt. The total company that migrated with him numbered about seventy souls. But at the point where the book of Exodus begins, more than two hundred years later, they had increased in number to around two millions.

Upon his arrival in Egypt, Israel was presented to Pharaoh who, for Joseph's sake, gave him and his sons the best of the land. They were settled in the territory of Goshen, which is sometimes also called Rameses. This was a fertile area, lying in lower Egypt, and situated to the east of the Nile delta. Later, Israel's people built the city of Rameses which, in all probability, served as the capital of the region.

We are not given the personal names of the Pharaohs referred to in the Biblical history. (Pharaoh was the title given to the kings of ancient Egypt.) Besides being different personalities, they may even have represented different dynasties in the long and eventful story of ancient Egypt. We do know, however, that the Pharaoh of the oppression was not the Pharaoh who had welcomed Israel and his sons and their families to Egypt, and given them the best of the land.

The People Oppressed

With the passage of time the favourable treatment that had been accorded them at the first began to change. Another king arose, maybe even another dynasty, and suspicions grew among the governing classes that in time of war, an alien people in their midst could become a kind of fifth column. Consequently, they lost their liberty and in the end they became cheap labour to build store cities for the Egyptians. It was in that servitude they came under the control of Pharaoh's taskmasters who cruelly oppressed them.

This cruel bondage had actually been anticipated some four hundred years before. In the everlasting covenant God had made with Abraham, the Lord said, "Know of a surety that your seed shall be a stranger in a land that is not theirs, and shall serve them; and they shall afflict them four hundred years; And also that nation, whom they shall serve, will I judge: and afterward shall they come out with great substance" (Gen.15:13,14).

The time had now come for that centuries old pledge to be honoured. And it was also time for the promise given to Jacob at Beersheba to be redeemed. "I will go down with you into Egypt; and I will also surely bring you up again" (Gen.46:4). The time had come for God to raise up a much needed deliverer to go before His people.

Besides being anticipated from the time of Abraham, their lot had also been the subject of God's overruling providence. In marvellous detail we are told how "He sent a man before them, even Joseph, who was sold for a servant ... the king sent and loosed him ... He made him lord of his house and ruler of all his substance ... Israel also came into Egypt ... He increased his people greatly, and made them stronger than their enemies. He turned their [the Egyptians] heart to hate the people, to deal subtly with his servants. He sent Moses, His servant, and Aaron, whom He had chosen" (Psalm 105:17-26).

Life in Egypt

In spite of this it would appear that their extended sojourn in Egypt had a pernicious and baneful effect on the people of Israel. They had even become worshippers of strange gods and heathen deities. Several years after the exodus, Joshua exhorted the nation, "Put away the gods which your fathers served ... in Egypt" (Josh.24:14). And Joshua would have known about this, for he lived in Egypt during the final stages of the servitude.

Moses, too, was born at that same time. But Moses parents had evidently kept themselves free from the prevailing idolatry, and had remained true to the faith of Abraham. Moses' father and mother, Amram and Jochebed, firmly believed that God would demonstrate plainly that however unfaithful His people proved themselves to be, He would remain true to His covenant promises.

The world upon which Moses first opened his eyes was clearly a hostile place. An anti-Semitic statute had been adopted by the Egyptian government. It required that all male children born to the Hebrews should be cast into the river. And yet, in a most extraordinary manner, Moses was preserved in those very waters that had destroyed so many. And in the strange and overruling providence of God, he actually came to reside in the Egyptian court for the first forty years of his life.

During those years he was instructed in all the wisdom of Egypt. He was cultivated in all the royal graces, and carefully groomed to succeed to the Egyptian throne. This meant that he would one day take the place of a king whose unswerving conviction was that the deities of his people stood universally supreme. And foremost among those deities was the celebrated Egyptian sun-god, housed in the famous Temple of Phthah, with its gorgeously sculptured galleries. In the context of such an exalted environment Moses must have developed into a very polished, and important person indeed.

A Mother's Influence

Unknown to the Egyptians, however, but clearly ordained by God, Pharaoh's palace during those early years had become an academy, in which this future deliverer of God's chosen people was tutored by his godly mother. Having been appointed his childhood nurse, she carefully instilled into his mind all the ways of Israel's God, and all the promises given to the fathers. Christian mothers today would do well to learn from Jochebed and prove in their own spheres, as she did in hers, that God still honours those who honour Him.

The record shows that when he was forty years old Moses fell from favour with Egypt's ruling elite. It happened because he had intervened and killed an Egyptian, who he came across oppressing an Israelite. This incident became the catalyst that brought into focus all the things he had been taught by his mother. It was probably the time of greatest crisis in his entire life. He had to choose between His people's God, and the tantalising prospects offered by Egypt.

Moses was faced with the most stupendous decision he would ever make. He chose wisely, and decided to renounce Egypt's quite substantial material advantages, for other and greater treasure. He esteemed the reproach of Christ greater riches than the treasures in Egypt. We are told that he forsook Egypt, not fearing the wrath of the king; for he endured, as seeing Him who is invisible. (See Hebs.11:24-27.)

Exile

Leaving Egypt, Moses sought refuge in the land of Midian, which lay to the west of the Gulf of Akaba and to the east of Mount Horeb. It was while in Midian, alone, and in exile, and resting one day by a well, that he found himself drawn into conflict. Seven young women came to draw water for their father's flock, but the local shepherds opposed them. Once again, Moses had to take sides and, instinctively, he stood up for the women and against the shepherds. In the end, one of those young women became his wife. Her name was Zipporah.

A further forty years is passed over in silence and then we find Moses tending his father-in-law's sheep in the Midian desert. "Moses kept the flock of Jethro, his father-in-law, the priest of Midian; and he led the flock to the [west side] of the desert, and came to the mount of God, even to Horeb" (Ex.3:1). Although passed over in silence, those years spent as a shepherd in the wilderness of Midian proved to be a magnificent preparation for the task God had for Moses to do. The second forty years of his life had been spent in a university, different from any in Egypt. He had been in God's school.

Stephen, the first Christian martyr, in his forthright defence before the Sanhedrin many years later, referred to that time. He told how "he [Moses] supposed his brethren would have understood how that God by his hand would deliver them." But Moses had to learn that deliverance would come, not from the east or from the west, nor by his own hand but by the hand of the angel who appeared to him in the bush. (See Acts 7: 25,35.) It took forty years for Moses to learn that the really important thing was not what he would do for God, but what God would do through him.

The Burning Bush

While tending his flock in the region of mount Horeb one day a flaming thorn bush caught Moses' attention. Although the bush burned it was not consumed and intrigued by this, he turned aside to investigate. As he did so a voice told him to take off his shoes for he was standing on holy ground. He soon became aware that he stood in the very presence of "the God of Abraham, the God of Isaac, and the God of Jacob" (Ex.3: 6).

This turning aside became another pivotal point in Moses' experience, for it was at this time he received his great commission. He was assigned the task of going back to Egypt to effect the deliverance of his people. Moreover, this was the occasion of an encounter with God, the reality of which he never forgot. Some forty years later, when he addressed his people for the last time, he still spoke of "the good will of Him who dwelt in the bush" (Deut.33:16).

In passing we might note that the burning bush speaks to us potently of the Lord Jesus Christ. As God dwelt in the bush, so "the Word was made flesh and dwelt among us" (John 1:14). And as God spoke through the bush, so "God ... has in these last days spoken unto us [in] His Son" (Hebs.1:2). Moreover, just as the bush was not consumed, so we read that the humanity of the Lord Jesus saw no corruption. (See Acts 2:27.)

Besides pointing us to Christ, however, the burning bush in all probability was also symbolic of the sufferings of the children of Israel. At that time their afflictions were great indeed, but so too was the preserving power of God. Their very continuance then, as indeed it also is today, was a testimony to the faithfulness of their covenant-keeping God. The history records, "The more they [the Egyptians] afflicted them, the more they [the Israelites] multiplied and grew" (Ex.1:12).

God's Purpose Revealed

Standing before that burning bush, Moses heard the God of his fathers speak in tones of tenderest love. The Lord disclosed to him in considerable detail His gracious purposes for His people. We must quote at length what was said on that memorable occasion. "And the Lord said, I have surely seen the affliction of my people who are in Egypt, and have heard their cry by reason of their taskmasters; for I know their sorrows; And I am come down to deliver them out of the hand of the Egyptians, and to bring them up out of that land unto a good and large land, unto a land flowing with milk and honey ... " (Ex.3:7,8).

Having been carefully instructed by his mother in the covenant promises, Moses understood the significance of these words. He knew that this was the long awaited signal that the promised deliverance was at last about to take place. Every word was in perfect accord with the covenant made with Abraham, and confirmed to Isaac and yet again to Jacob. Moreover, the whole statement was directly relevant to his oppressed people's need. What was about to happen must have surpassed even their best imaginings.

The Gospel of our Salvation

The message Moses received at Horeb was also a trailblazer of the gospel of our salvation through Christ. The thing that really stands out is that God had come down in grace to deliver His people. Later, when the tabernacle would be set up, God would come down in glory to dwell among His people. These two significant things mark the perimeters of the book of Exodus. They probably find their New Testament answer first, in the coming of the Saviour and then in the coming of the Spirit at Pentecost.

In the deliverance announced through the burning bush, we are able to hear an echo of the angels' message to the Bethlehem shepherds at the time of our Saviour's birth. "For unto you is born this day in the city of David a Saviour, who is Christ the Lord" (Luke 2:11). In language almost identical to what Moses heard, the Lord Jesus said, "I am come that they might have life, and that they might have it more abundantly" (John 10:10). And again, "The Son of man is come to seek and to save that which was lost" (Luke 19:10).

At Horeb Moses was told that the deliverance, when it came, would effectively be in three parts. His people would be brought out of Egypt, through the wilderness, and finally, they would be brought into the promised land. Like theirs, ours too is a threefold salvation. We have been saved from the penalty of sin, we are being saved from the power of sin, and one day we shall be saved from the very presence of sin. One writer very appropriately designated this, "So great salvation" (Hebs.2:3).

In the first instance, therefore, the message of the burning bush was to Moses and to his people, but it has a secondary application to us as well. How often in seasons of distress we have fallen back on the verbs of that wonderful statement. "I have surely seen the affliction of my people ... and I have heard their cry ... for I know their sorrows" (Ex.3:7). While this scripture may not be about us, but about God's people in another age, who can doubt that it is for us? Let no one rob us of its comfort.

Chapter 2
The Vital Difference

Fear not; for I have redeemed you.
Isa. 43:1.

Passing over much varied and meaningful detail about Moses' experiences when he returned to Egypt, we come to the deliverance itself. Nine judgement plagues fell upon Egypt in quick succession, profoundly impacting the land. Then the crunch came; there would be one more plague. But before the tenth and final plague the Lord said He would put a difference between the Egyptians and the Israelites. "That you may know how that the Lord does put a difference between the Egyptians and Israel" (Ex.11:7).

Redemption

The specific term used here for 'difference' is in some Bible margins rendered 'redemption.' A redemption was about to take place that would put a difference between some people who would be saved, and other people who would perish. That redemption, of course, was a figure of a far greater redemption. It pointed forward to the sacrifice of Calvary when Christ "obtained eternal redemption for us"(Hebs.9:12).

Like oxygen in the air, this arresting subject pervades the Word of God. In the Old Testament we have the witness of Job, who is believed to have been a contemporary of Abraham, a witness who surely carried his own conviction. He said, "I know that my Redeemer lives" (Job 19:25). Turning to the New Testament we read, "When the fullness of the time was come, God sent forth His Son ... to redeem" (Gal.4:4,5).

And these are just two references chosen from a multitude of similar quotes on this marvellous theme. Besides imbuing the sacred writings, the subject of redemption has also filled the hymn-books of the Christian church through the ages, and it has singularly warmed the hearts of believers across the generations. Charles Wesley who, it was claimed, gave to the English-speaking world its richest heritage of sacred song, wrote thus:

O for a thousand tongues to sing
My great Redeemer's praise,
The glories of my God and King,
The triumphs of His grace!

Redemption has two criteria at its root. In the first place it means to buy or to buy back, and secondly, it means to set free. In scripture, therefore, it is presented both as a price needing to be paid, and as a power needing to be displayed. In the case of the children of Israel, they were not only redeemed from the judgement of God, they were also set free from the dominion of Pharaoh. The former involved the death of the passover lamb, and the latter the putting forth of divine power in a way not previously seen.

The Passover

The final Egyptian plague would involve the death of every firstborn throughout all the land, from the king in his palace to the felon in his prison. At midnight the destroying angel would pass through the land, and the firstborn would be slain. But a way of deliverance had been divinely revealed, and Moses proclaimed it to his people. In the tenth day of the month every household must take a lamb; a lamb for a house. After three days, during which time it's suitability would have been proved, the lamb was to be killed, and it's blood sprinkled on the lintel and the doorposts of their houses.

The Witness to the Lamb

To say that the whole Bible is the story of the lamb, is not to overstate the case. To Cain and Abel, the first children of our first parents, God had made known a way back to Himself from the dark paths of sin. It was through the slain lamb and the shed blood. And when, at length, the Lord of Glory appeared in human form to put away sin, the forerunner identified Him, as "The Lamb of God, who takes away the sin of the world" (John 1:29).

Three quarters of a millennium before the cross, Isaiah had insisted on the personality of God's lamb. He wrote, "He is brought as a lamb to the slaughter, and as a sheep before her shearers is dumb, so he openeth not his mouth" (Isa.53:7). And in the New Testament Philip, the evangelist, was quick to show the ambassador from Ethiopia how this prophecy was fulfilled in Christ. (See Acts 8:32.)

We are told in the book of Revelation, that when the apostle John was caught up into heaven, and saw the throne of God, this is what he noted, "I beheld and, lo, in the midst of the throne ... stood a lamb as though it had been slain." (See Rev.5:6.) At the beginning of the Bible and at its end, as well as all the way through, we have this constant witness to the lamb.

With great clarity, the apostle Peter proclaimed the dying of God's Lamb, and the shedding of His precious blood, as the only basis of our redemption. He wrote in unambiguous terms, "Forasmuch as you know that you were not redeemed with corruptible things, like silver and gold ... But with the precious blood of Christ, as of a lamb without blemish and without spot" (1Pet.1:18,19).

We certainly have substantial grounds for transferring the various aspects of the passover story to ourselves, and to our Saviour's redeeming work. Our authority is plainly stated in the epistle where we read, "For even Christ, our passover, is sacrificed for us" (1Cor.5:7). In all generations spiritual minds have discerned in the passover lamb precious insights into the character of our Lord Jesus Christ. The lamb's every detail is like a fingerpost pointing forward to Him.

When I see the blood

Just before that first passover the Lord gave a promise to Moses that must have been uncommonly precious in the ears of every Israelite. It would have struck a chord of blessed assurance. The Lord said, "When I see the blood, I will pass [hover] over you, and the plague shall not be upon you to destroy you, when I smite the land of Egypt" (Ex.12:13). That pledge would enable the children of Israel, to anticipate that fateful midnight hour in Egypt, with calm assurance and quiet confidence. Without fear or trepidation, they could rest on the Lord's word and be heartened by it.

We, too, have been given exceeding great and precious promises. (See 2Pet.1:4.) For instance, we have the unequivocal testimony of scripture to the precious blood of Christ. "In [Him] we have redemption through His blood, the forgiveness of sins, according to the riches of His grace" (Eph.1:7). Because we are in Christ, as all the firstborn of Israel were in houses sprinkled with the blood, we have both redemption and the forgiveness of sins. Our enjoyment of these things and our peace, is found in simply resting on what God says in His word.

How calm the judgement hour shall pass,
For all who do obey,
The word of God, and trust the blood,
And make that word their stay.

The Exodus

New Beginning

The passover not only brought the Egyptian servitude to an end, it also signalled the beginning of a long and eventful journey for the people newly redeemed. And, in addition, it signalled an important change in their calendar. Israel's new year would no longer begin with the month Tishri, sometimes called Ethanim, the month of harvest, but with Abib, the month of green ears. (Many years later, following the captivity in Babylon, Abib became known as Nisan.)

In an ongoing way this change in the calendar would be very significant for the redeemed people. It would be a perpetual reminder to them that redemption lay at the centre of their new relationship with the Lord. Throughout their history every new year would henceforth be illumined by the memory of the Lord's passover and of their deliverance from Egypt.

Hasty Summons

Early in the morning following the passover, Pharaoh and his people pressed the children of Israel to take their flocks and their herds, and begone; for they said, "We are all dead men." This meant that in the end the exodus was a hasty affair. "And they baked unleavened cakes ... it was not leavened, because they were thrust out of Egypt, and could not tarry" (Ex.12:39).

In fact, there were three dimensions to Israel's exodus. We know that God brought them out. This is repeatedly stressed in scripture. The people were even charged at the time to teach this to their children. "By strength of hand the Lord brought us out from Egypt, from the house of bondage" (Ex.13:14). God brought them out, and Pharaoh thrust them out, but we are also told that they went out. Of their own voluntary will they turned their backs on Egypt. The psalmist, emphasising this particular dimension, declared "When Israel went out of Egypt, the house of Jacob from a people of strange language" (Psa.114:1).

These things have their counterpart in our own spiritual experience as well. We readily concede that our salvation was all of God. It was God who saved us. But after that we soon began to feel that we no longer belonged in this world; it seemed that the world itself had become alien to us, and we to it. We had become strangers and pilgrims in the earth. (See 1Peter 2:11.) And then we heard the Saviour's call, Follow me, and of our own volition we responded, and like Israel leaving Egypt, we separated ourselves unto Him, bearing His reproach.

Succoth - the first encampment

Leaving Rameses the people came to Succoth where they lodged in makeshift dwellings or booths. It is an interesting detail that even down to this day, when Jewish people keep the feast of tabernacles they will often vacate their regular houses, and move into temporary booths, for the seven days of the feast. In this way they keep alive the memory of their forefathers' release from Egypt and the time of their first encampment at Succoth. (See Lev. 23:41,42.)

(i) Unleavened Bread
Two ordinances were established at Succoth. The first was the feast of unleavened bread. This was intrinsically connected with the observance of the passover, for passover was also the first day of unleavened bread. Just as Passover stands for redemption, so Unleavened Bread represents the life of the redeemed.

This was a seven day feast, and in preparation for it, all traces of leaven were painstakingly purged from their dwellings. In the New Testament, leaven is consistently used as a figure of what is evil. (See 1Cor.5:8.) The parable of the three measures of meal (See Matt.13:33.) is sometimes thought to be an exception to this rule, but when rightly understood it actually confirms the principle. Unleavened bread, therefore, proclaims the redeemed person's life as a life of separation from evil, not just for one day of the week, but for every day.

(ii) The Firstborn
The other matter established at Succoth was the setting apart of the firstborn for the Lord. The principle proclaimed at Succoth was this, "Every firstling ... shall be the Lord's" (Ex.13:12). The slaying of the firstborn of the Egyptians, and the sanctifying of the firstborn of the Israelites, combined to emphasise the claims of God. It is a principle that holds to this day, for the Lord still has claims upon the lives of His people. An ancient proverb says, "Honour the Lord with your substance, and with the firstfruits of all your increase" (Prov.3:9).

The tribe of Levi was later substituted for the firstborn of all the families of Israel. The Lord said "The Levites shall be mine. They are wholly given unto me from among the children of Israel" (Num.8:14,16). In this way the Levites took the place of all who had been delivered from death by the blood of the slain lamb. Levi was then chosen to become the priestly tribe, and was made responsible for the proper functioning of the tabernacle, and the carrying through of its various services.

Later still, when the land of Canaan was divided among the tribes, no inheritance was given to the Levites. "Levi has no part nor inheritance with his brethren; the Lord is his inheritance" (Deut.10:9). But the Levites were given forty-eight cities, including the six cities of refuge. Significantly, these cities were scattered throughout all the tribes. This may well have been what Jacob meant when he spoke prophetically of Levi, "I will divide them in Jacob, and scatter them in Israel" (Gen.49:7).

The Guidance of God

In addition to these two ordinances, a third thing is mentioned in connection with Succoth. For the first time, we read of the pillar of cloud by day, and of fire by night. This was God's gift to His people for their guidance. The redeemed were not left to their own devices. "The Lord went before them by day in a pillar of cloud, to lead them the way; and by night in a pillar of fire, to give them light; to go by day and night: He took not away the pillar of cloud by day, nor the pillar of fire by night, from before the people" (Ex.13:21,22). We shall consider the significance of the cloudy pillar more fully in a later chapter.

Chapter 3
Delivered from Pharaoh's Power

He led them forth by the right way.
Psa.107:7.

From Succoth the children of Israel moved on to a position between Migdol and the Red Sea. The stage was now set for the other side of their redemption to be accomplished. On the human level their new position was a rather disingenuous choice of location. They were surrounded by the wilderness, they had mountains on either side of them, and before them lay the sea. They found themselves in what appeared to be a rather invidious cul-de-sac.

Yet they were there in the will of God and the narrative shows that the Lord had a predetermined purpose in bringing His people to that unpromising place. In fact, the whole scene is a notable example of how God moves in mysterious ways, His wonders to perform. The record stands as an enduring testimony to the Lord's care for His own.

There was a nearer way, but He who knows the end from the beginning, knew the dangers it held. He also knew His people through and through, and He knew that they were not yet ready to face those dangers. We are comforted by the knowledge that with the same watchfulness the Lord leads His people still. "For He knows our frame; He remembers that we are dust" (Psa.103:14).

Pharaoh Enticed

It is not surprising that Pharaoh saw in their parlous situation an opportunity to bring the Israelites once more under his control. It seemed that they had lost their way, and had become entangled in the wilderness. The Egyptian king was sure that nothing could rescue these fugitives, hampered as they were with large numbers of women and children. He would quickly reassert his authority over the people he had oppressed for so long.

Having recovered somewhat from the effects of the final plague, Pharaoh decided to pursue his prey. "The Egyptians pursued after them, all the horses and chariots of Pharaoh, and his horsemen, and his army, and overtook them encamping by the sea" (Ex.14:9). But the Lord, who had brought Israel out of Egypt, and guided them to this place, was also in control of their destiny. He would entice Pharaoh and his armies to their destruction. And in this unlikely place He would fulfil His declared purpose for the people He had redeemed.

The experts are divided in their attempts to pinpoint the precise spot where it all happened. But we know that a way was miraculously opened for Moses and his people to pass through the sea as on dry land. Presumptuously, their pursuers decided to follow them, and while they were still in the sea, the Lord took off the wheels of the Egyptian chariots. And when it was too late to call a retreat, the Lord commanded Moses to stretch out his hand over the sea so that the waters returned to their strength.

Needless to say, the waters rolled over the Egyptians and they were drowned, and the next morning their dead bodies were washed up on the shore. The history records, "Thus the Lord saved Israel that day out of the hand of the Egyptians; and Israel saw the Egyptians dead upon the seashore. And Israel saw that great work which the Lord did upon the Egyptians: and the people feared the Lord, and believed the Lord and His servant Moses" (Ex.14:30,31).

Deliverance

We should pay attention to the conclusion that was reached in the final report: "Thus the Lord saved Israel that day out of the hand of the Egyptians" (Ex.14:30). The word 'thus' refers, not just to the fact of their deliverance, but also to the manner of it. God had been acting all along in a way consistent with His own character. His understanding of everyone involved in the great drama says a lot about His mercy and His wisdom.

Pharaoh was the chief protagonist. Can anyone doubt that he had been given ample opportunity to avoid the suffering that had come upon his people? Before its display in the happenings at the Red Sea, the power of Jehovah had been clearly demonstrated in the plagues that had fallen on Egypt. But Pharaoh had hardened his heart. And in the end God hardened Pharaoh's heart. As for the children of Israel, they had nothing to glory in except the Lord. For their deliverance had been effected, not by their own exertions, but by His stretched out arm alone.

There are many striking parallels between Israel's deliverance and what has been accomplished for us in the dying and rising again of the Lord Jesus Christ. On the farther shore of the Red Sea, the children of Israel could only stand back and exclaim, "Not unto us, O Lord, not unto us, but unto thy name give glory" (Psa.115:1). And we who stand on the resurrection side of Calvary's cross, can only bow our heads in deep humility and say, "According as it is written, He that glories, let him glory in the Lord" (1Cor.1:31). In fact, every age has had to confess that "Salvation is of the Lord" (Jonah 2:9).

For our part, we know that just as the power of Pharaoh and of Egypt was broken at the Red Sea, so the power of Satan and of sin was broken by the Lord Jesus in His cross. "Having spoiled principalities and powers, He made a show of them openly, triumphing over them in [the cross]" (Col.2:15). After the Red Sea, Pharaoh could no longer claim any dominion over Israel; nor can Satan today have any claim upon believers in the risen Lord Jesus. Hence it is written, "If the Son, therefore, shall make you free, you shall be free indeed" (John 8:36).

Free to Serve God

But the people of Israel had not been set free to do their own thing. When at the first, Moses stood before Pharaoh he demanded his people's freedom in these terms: "Thus says the Lord, Let my people go, that they may serve me" (Ex.8:1). They had not been free to serve God in Egypt, certainly not according to His purpose for them, but now they were free indeed.

Delivered from the house of bondage and the yoke of Pharaoh, they were now free to serve the living and the true God. And like Israel after the Red Sea, we too are free, we are free from the enslaving power of sin, but we are not free to do our own thing. The tyranny of self would not be freedom. But we have been set free to walk with Christ in a new kind of life, and to serve Him all our days.

The parallel between them and us is really very precise. Paul wrote, "All our fathers were under the cloud, and all passed through the sea. And were all baptised unto Moses in the cloud and in the sea" (1Cor.10:1,2). This has its modern counterpart in Christian baptism. Going down into the waters of baptism, believers signify their identification with Christ in His death; and coming up again, they signify their identification with Him in His resurrection.

Our New Position

It is so important for us to grasp our new position following conversion. God now looks on us as having died with Christ, and as having been raised again with Him. "Knowing this, that our old man was crucified with Him, that the body of sin might be [unemployed], that henceforth we should not serve sin" (Rom.6:6). This is the primary idea symbolically expressed in the baptismal act.

The practical expression of these things in the believer's personal life, however, must be a matter of faith. For the scripture goes on to say, "Likewise, reckon ye also yourselves to be dead indeed unto sin, but alive unto God through Jesus Christ, our Lord. Let not sin, therefore, reign in your mortal body, that you should obey it in its lusts. Neither yield your members as instruments of unrighteousness unto sin, but yield yourselves unto God, as those that are alive from the dead, and your members as instruments of righteousness unto God" (Rom.6:11-13).

The expression of these things in a life of faith is the very essence of true Christian experience. And in the next stage of this incredible journey, these things will be powerfully brought to our notice, and their significance will be explained in quite considerable detail.

When we walk with the Lord,
 In the light of His word,
What a glory He sheds on our way!
While we do His good will
He abides with us still,
And with all who will Trust and Obey.

Stage Two
The Life of Faith
(From the Red Sea to Sinai)

Chapter 4
Across the Sea

He made known His ways unto Moses, His acts unto the
children of Israel. Psa. 103:7.

With the overthrow of Pharaoh an entirely new vista opened up
before the children of Israel. Besides enticing Egypt's armies to
their destruction, the Lord had important things to teach His people.
And their education in those things was scheduled to begin
immediately at the Red Sea. Basic to everything else was the
importance of faith. In all His dealings with them, the Lord's
primary purpose would now be to develop and strengthen their
faith.

Since the principle of faith is as pertinent to us as it was to them, it
is vital for us to recognise that the great issues of faith transcend
all the dispensations, they are the same in every age. We rightly
make much of the fact that we are saved by faith, but now we must
learn to walk by faith. "Without faith it is impossible to please
God; for he that comes to God must believe that He is, and that He
is a rewarder of them that dilligently seek Him" (Hebs.11:6).

Real Life Situations

Because faith is so pivotal to the spiritual life, the Lord resolved
that Israel should learn its implications in the context of real life
situations, rather than in a merely theoretical way. However, it is
extremely doubtful if the people ever really understood this, and
their very dullness is a challenge to us. How true it is that like

them, we too can pass through the most severe testings without deriving any real spiritual profit from the experience.

Time and again the Lord brought them under intense pressures of one kind and another. They were caused to feel the pangs of hunger and of thirst, and at times they even despaired of life itself. "Then they cried unto the Lord in their trouble, and He delivered them out of their distresses. And He led them forth by the right way, that they might go to a city of habitation" (Psa.107:6,7).

They witnessed the mighty works of the Lord at the Red Sea, and during their time in the wilderness. But it is not unreasonable to conclude that only Moses, and perhaps a few others, had the discernment necessary to see the principles underlying those mighty works. This seems to be the thought behind the scripture which says, "He made known His ways unto Moses, His acts unto the children of Israel" (Psa.103:7).

They could marvel at His deliverances, and many times they would say, "Oh, that men would praise the Lord for His goodness, and for His wonderful works to the children of men!" (Psa.107:8,15,21,31) But for all that, they never seemed to quite understand the ways of God. It is clear that they saw His acts, but it is equally clear that they profited little from what they saw.

The Near Way

Having just emerged from a lifetime of slavery and deprivation, the children of Israel were in urgent need of discipline and training. They had never before known the freedom they now enjoyed. For that reason "God led them not through the way of the land of the Philistines, although that was near" (Ex.13:17). Admittedly, the long way round had its difficulties, but had they gone by the near way, they would have been precipitated into problems for which they were wholly unprepared.

The inspired comment on Israel's exodus is rather telling. "He led them forth by the right way, that they might go to a city of habitation" (Psa.107:7). Their experience teaches us that the near way is not always the best way. It is so important to remember this, especially when the Lord seems to be leading us in what appear to be roundabout ways. Since His ways are all wise, we can be confident that the Lord will not direct our steps into any danger without some prior preparation.

However perplexing our path at times may be, we should be mindful of His word which says, "For my thoughts are not your thoughts, neither are your ways my ways, saith the Lord. For as the heavens are higher than the earth, so are my ways higher than your ways, and my thoughts than your thoughts" (Isa.55:8,9). Out of a wealth of personal experience, David the Psalmist, wrote: "He leads me in [right] paths for His name's sake" (Psa.23:3).

As we walk in His ways therefore, the Lord will surely preserve us from ills beyond our endurance. He has said, "There has no temptation taken you but such as is common to man; but God is faithful, who will not suffer you to be tempted above that you are able, but will, with the temptation, also make a way to escape, that you may be able to bear it" (1Cor.10:13).

Preparation for Life

The present difficulties of our path, are probably just a preparation for other situations, as yet unknown, which we must inevitably face. We have already noted this very principle in the life of Moses. The forty years spent in Midian, with all their privations and fustrations, were the divinely appointed preparation for him to lead God's people in their incredible journey. And even at this point in the journey, as we shall see, God was already preparing a successor to Moses in the person of Joshua. A through understanding of this principle will help us to face the future in a way that might otherwise be quite impossible.

Two Resources of Faith

The children of Israel were now engaged, on the basis of a living faith, to walk with the Lord across a trackless desert. As a priority, they will need to understand that faith has just two resources, namely (i) God Himself and (ii) His Word. These were Noah's resources when he built the ark. It was just the same with Abraham when he left Mesopotamia to go into Canaan. Now, it would be no different for Moses and his people as they set out on their incredible journey.

But, as we have noted, the generation that came out of Egypt was slow to appreicate these things. Instead of trusting Him we are told: "They tempted God ... Yea, they spoke against God; they said, Can God furnish a table in the wilderness" (Psa.78:18,19). The New Testament discloses that it was their unbelief that prevented them from entering Canaan: unbelief was the reason why they perished in the wilderness.

It was by faith they are said to have passed through the Red Sea as on dry land. But the really significant thing, which we must carefully note, is that the next recorded evidence of faith in action was at Jericho, some forty years later, when the walls came tumbling down. (See Hebs.11:29,30.) It seems that at every turn they needed to learn over and over again the meaning of faith, even in its most elementary forms.

Two Aspects of Faith

At the Red Sea they were also taught that there are two sides to faith. At times faith is passive, and at other times it is active. Distinguishing between these two features of faith will always require great discernment and a deep exercise of heart. Abraham and Isaac, together on mount Moriah illustrate both kinds of faith.

Abraham's faith was of the active sort. He rose early to cleave the wood and saddle the ass. When they came to the place, it was Abraham who built the altar, and bound Isaac, and laid him on the altar. But in Isaac we see faith in its passive aspect. Isaac allowed himself to be bound; he allowed himself to be laid on the altar. The marvellous thing is that God honoured both the passive faith of

Isaac and the active faith of Abraham.

Passive faith

At the Red Sea, when the children of Israel looked and saw Pharaoh and his hosts pursuing them from behind, they cried out in fear. But Moses quietly turned to the Lord. He would learn from the Lord what the people must do. The first charge God gave them called forth a passive faith. "Fear not, stand still, and see the salvation of the Lord" (Ex.14:13). They must wait upon God. And experience teaches us that this is the first attribute of faith.

Unlike his predecessor, who preferred to do his own thing, David was content to wait upon the Lord. In the psalms he repeatedly urged this on men and women of faith in every generation. He said, Wait on the Lord ... Wait, I say, on the Lord" (Psa.27:14). Isaiah added this reassuring note, "They that wait upon the Lord shall renew their strength; they shall mount up with wings as eagles; they shall run, and not be weary; and they shall walk, and not faint" (Isa.40:31).

Active faith

But the Lord's second instruction was entirely different. "Speak unto the children of Israel, that they go forward" (Ex.14:15). The need now was for an active faith. The narrative, records how they went forward, and it shows how God honoured them as they went. And at the same time He honoured His word, for the people were miraculously delivered from their foes. The first charge called for something they could easily do, they could stand still, but the second charge called for something that required the intervention of God.

Both these charges were laid upon the man with the paralysed hand in the synagogue at Capernaum. (See Mark3:1.) In the first instance the Lord told him to Stand forth. This was something he could easily do, and he did it. Then he was told, Stretch forth your hand. This was not so easy, but as he obeyed he received strength to do what hitherto he had found it impossible to do. That is how faith operated at the Red Sea and at Capernaum, and in principle, its operation is still like that today. The Lord always gives the needed enablement for us to do what He commands.

The Song of Deliverance

It was a truly exhilarating moment for the children of Israel when they stood on the wilderness shore of the Red Sea. It was a moment of glorious vision. "Israel saw that great work which the Lord did upon the Egyptians" (Ex.14:31). Having witnessed such an astonishing display of God's power, they could now look forward to the further outworking of His plans. He would bring them to their promised haven, and establish them in the land of their desire. If God was for them, who could be against them?

This was a moment to be savoured, and they rightly lifted up their voices in thanksgiving. With one heart and voice, and without reserve, they sung the song of Moses. "I will sing unto the Lord, for He has triumphed gloriously: the horse and his rider has He thrown into the sea" (Ex.15:1).

It was a glad and jubilant paean of praise; a finely tuned expression of gratitude to God for such a spectacular manifestation of His goodness. Their plight had been extreme indeed but the Lord had been their strength and He had brought them through in triumph. At the Red Sea Pharoah had been given the final answer to his proud retort at the first. "Who is the Lord, that I should obey His voice to let Israel go?" With all their hearts they must sing unto the Lord.

Herbert Lockyer told of a function in a London girl's school many years ago. In full voice the choir rendered: "All hail the power of Jesus' name!" Present was Adolph Monod the father of one of the girls. Quite overcome with emotion, the great theologian said afterwards, "My weak heart gave way, and I could not but weep instead of singing. The whole of sacred criticism is not worth my little girl of six years old, opening her mouth and saying to angels, to Jews, Gentiles and Christians - "Crown Him Lord of all!"

O that with yonder sacred throng
We at His feet may fall!
Join in the everlasting song,
And crown Him Lord of all!

Chapter 5
We Walk by Faith

Without faith it is impossible to please Him.
Hebs.11:6.

Israel's singing before long gave way to sighing. From the sea they moved on to a place called Marah, which means bitter. Being thirsty, they hastened to drink of the water that was there. But the water at Marah was the brackish water of the Red Sea. Probably it had seeped through the ground and gathered in this hollow spot in the wilderness. It was so bitter they could not drink it. What would they do? What about the women and the children? Their disappointment soon boiled over and their impulsive reaction was to murmur against Moses, but his reaction was always to wait upon the Lord.

Two Characteristics of Faith

Even in this situation the Lord was seeking to progress the people's spiritual education. Since the two resources of faith are God Himself and His word, it follows that the two characteristics of faith are dependence on God and obedience to His word. These are the things God would teach His people at Marah and not only at Marah, but the whole journey through.

Dependence
At Marah, the people had to learn again their dependence on God. They had no resources of their own and Marah simply revealed this weakness and proved that the wilderness could not supply their need. They must look up to the God who had delivered them from Egypt, who had brought them through the sea and who had

pledged to bring them to the promised land.

"The Lord showed him [Moses] a tree, which when he had cast into the waters, the waters were made sweet" (Ex.15:25). Spiritual minds have always seen in that tree, a type of the Saviour, who was cut off out of the land of the living. The spiritual lesson for our souls is fairly obvious. As Moses brought that tree into the bitter waters of Marah, so we must bring the Lord into all our disappointments. To do so is to find that He sweetens every bitter cup. Prayer enables us to do this, for prayer is an expression of our dependence on God. Prayer is the exercise that opens the door and admits the Lord to our areas of need.

Oh what peace we often forfeit,
Oh what needless pain we bear,
All because we do not carry
Everything to God in prayer.

Obedience
The second characteristic of faith is obedience! This too, was on the curriculum at Marah. The Lord established an ordinance there, He said, "If you will diligently hearken unto the voice of the Lord your God, and will do that which is right in His sight, and will give ear to His commandments, and keep all His statutes, I will put none of these diseases upon you, which I have brought upon the Egyptians; for I am the Lord that heals you" (Ex.15:26). These words remind us of how the Lord Jesus said to the disciples, "If you love me, keep my commandments" (John 14:15).

It is clear from both parts of scripture that the living God attaches supreme importance to His will being done in earth, as it is in heaven. We have seen how Pharaoh had just proved, to his own destruction, that God's will cannot be set aside with impunity. The story of the elect nation from then until now, has been a catalogue of severe chastening. And for what reason? Simply because the people persistently failed in this matter of obedience to the Lord. Isaiah emphasised this, "Oh, that you had hearkened to my commandments! Then had your peace been like a river, and your righteousness like the waves of the sea" (Isa. 48:18).

Both these characteristics of faith are helpfully brought together in the familiar lines -

Trust and obey;
For there's no other way,
To be happy in Jesus,
But to trust and obey.

An Oasis

From Marah the people journeyed to Elim. This was an oasis in the desert. It was an idyllic spot. There were twelve wells of water and seventy palm trees at Elim. They could lie on hammocks, strung between a couple of palm trees, and sip the sweet water from Elim's wells. They could relax at Elim for there were no pressures on them in that leafy place.

This, of course, must have been a welcome respite from the exertions they had been through. But we do not read of any profit for their souls at Elim. They did not sense any need there, nor did they prove the Lord's grace and power. Moreover, they did not see any of the acts of God there, and much less did they learn more of His ways.

The next two points on their journey brought them to, (i) the wilderness of Sin (Ex.16) and (ii) the valley of Rephidim (Ex.17). In the former they first received the manna to eat, and in the latter the Lord gave them water from the smitten rock to quench their thirst. In both these situations they wonderfully proved the goodness and mercy of their God. The necessities of life were in short supply in that inhospitable and arid desert, but this was simply an opportunity for the Lord to show them that He could meet their need.

The Manna

In the giving and receiving of the manna they were also taught the importance of dependence and obedience. The manna was given and gathered on a daily basis. If someone gathered more than a daily portion, perhaps enough to see them through the next day as well, that night it bred worms and stank. The manna was not given to be stored, it was given to be used, and used on a daily basis. This called for the exercise of a daily dependence on God to supply their need. The life of faith is like that, it is a daily experience of trust in God.

I would not ask for earthly store;
Thou wilt my need supply.
But I would covet, more and more,
The clear and single eye,
To see my duty face to face,
And trust thee, Lord, for daily grace.

On the sixth day, however, they were taught something of the other characteristic of faith. On that day they were told to gather a double portion of the manna. In view of what had happened when they gathered the double portion on an earlier day, some might have argued against this command. But the instruction they received called for a simple and specific obedience because the manna was not given on the sabbath or seventh day.

That the manna prefigured the Lord Jesus is repeatedly stressed in the New Testament. Jesus Himself said, "Your fathers did eat manna in the wilderness, and are dead ... I am the living bread that came down from heaven; if any man shall eat of this bread, he shall live forever" (John 6:49-51). Even the minutiae of the manna, its size, its shade and its shape, in fact its every detail, like every detail of the passover lamb, speaks to us of the unique person of our Saviour.

The manna first came down from heaven, and lay upon the face of the wilderness. Then a portion of it was stored, as a memorial, in a golden pot. This pot was eventually deposited in the Ark of the

Covenant. And since the Ark stood in the most holy place, the immediate presence of God, the stored manna was said to have been laid up before the Lord (Ex.16:33).

In all these details we are able to discern types or pictures of the Lord Jesus. In the manna coming down from heaven, we are able to see His coming into this world. The manna upon the face of the wilderness reminds us of our Saviour's pathway through this scene. And then, the manna laid up before the Lord presages how He went back into heaven. The apostle Peter declared, "God has made that same Jesus ... both Lord and Christ" (Acts 2:36). The story of the manna, therefore, brings us ultimately to the great truth of the Lordship of Christ.

Two Pillars of Faith

On the other hand, the valley of Rephidim and the water that flowed from the smitten rock bring us to that other foundation truth, the Gift of the Spirit. These two truths are really the two sides of the same coin. The Lordship of Christ, is the objective side of things and the Gift of the Spirit, is the subjective side. Taken together these two truths are the pillars upon which a strong faith can be built. Men and women of faith in every age have found it so.

The Lord Jesus promised His disciples, "I will pray the Father, and He shall give you another Comforter, that He may abide with you forever; even the Spirit of truth" (John 14:16,17). This promise accorded with another assertion from our Lord's lips. "In the last day, that great day of the feast, Jesus stood and cried, saying, If any man thirst, let him come unto me, and drink. He that believeth on me, as the scripture has said, out of his [heart] shall flow rivers of living water. (But this spoke He of the Spirit, whom they that believe on Him should receive; for the Holy Spirit was not yet given, because Jesus was not yet glorified)" (John 7:37-39).

The promise was fulfilled at Pentecost when the Holy Spirit was given to indwell believers. And we should note that the Holy Spirit was only given after the Saviour had first been 'smitten of God' and then raised from the dead and glorified. Israel drinking of the water that flowed from the smitten rock in Rephidim clearly forshadowed these things. For at Rephidim the order was exactly the same, the water was only given after the rock had first been smitten.

Because Calvary and Pentecost, in that order, are now historical facts, today's believers in the Lord Jesus receive the gift of the indwelling Holy Spirit at the point of conversion. "Peter said unto them, Repent, and be baptised, every one of you, in the name of Jesus Christ for the remission of sins, and you shall receive the gift of the Holy Spirit" (Acts 2:38). Later, when the people of Israel crossed over the river Arnon, they were given water to drink from the springing well of Beer. (See Num.21:16-18.) But the message there seems to be about the fullness of the Spirit being our enjoyed portion. The water from the smitten rock in Rephidim is about the Gift of the Spirit.

Chapter 6

Rephidim - The First Battle

Who, through faith, subdued kingdoms.
Hebs.11:33.

Since the Christian life is a life of constant conflict we can never afford to relax our guard, and this is particularly true should we be still relishing the afterglow of some special blessing. For at such a time an enemy will often seek us out. Abram found it so. Returning from a commanding victory in the war of the kings he was intercepted by the king of Sodom, who came with some very tempting offers. Happily, Abram had been prepared in advance through a prior meeting with Melchizedek, the priest, who was also the king of Salem.

War with Amalek

Another notable instance of this hostile tactic is found here at Rephidim. It was just at such a moment, that Israel's first enemy chose to launch an attack. "Then came Amalek, and fought with Israel in Rephidim" (Ex.17:8). The later history shows that Amalek continued to be an implacable foe, ever ready to strike at the people of Israel, especially in times of national weakness. When this first encounter ended in Amalek's defeat, the Lord swore that He will "have war with Amalek from generation to generation" (Ex.17:16).

Some years later Balaam was moved to declare, "Amalek was the first of the nations; but his latter end shall be that he perish forever" (Num.24:20). The expression the first of the nations did not mean that Amalek was preeminent among the nations of that region, a kind of superpower of the time. It meant rather that since the encounter in the valley of Rephidim was the first such attack, Amalek had become known as Israel's number one enemy.

The various references to Amalek, who was a descendant of Esau, leave us in no doubt that Amalek is a type of the flesh. "For the flesh lusts against the Spirit, and the Spirit against the flesh" (Gal.5:17). The universal experience of believers throughout the ages has been that the enmity between flesh and Spirit continues without remission like the war between Amalek and Israel from generation to generation. This first attack and its very timing is recorded as a salutary warning to all who tread the heavenly path.

Two Arenas of Faith

The war with Amalek graphically illustrates the two arenas where faith must operate. One is public, and the other private. The public arena is seen in Joshua fighting in the valley. Because the Christian life is a life of conflict, the language of the New Testament is frequently the language of conflict. For instance, we are urged to be strong in the grace that is in Christ Jesus, and again, to endure hardness as good soldiers of Jesus Christ. (See 2Tim.2:1-4.) We are also exhorted to "Put on the whole armour of God, that we may be able to stand against the wiles of the devil" (Eph.6:11).

The encounter with Amalek was very far from being a pushover. On the contrary, the battle raged to and fro. Sometimes Israel was in the ascendency, and then at other times it was Amalek. What Joshua did not realise at the time, although it was impressed upon him afterwards, was that the battle in the valley was actually determined by what was happening elsewhere. Another drama was taking place away from the scene of the fighting. And this brings us to the other arena where faith must operate.

Moses had ascended the mount, where he lifted up holy hands in intercession. While Moses' hands were raised, Joshua prevailed. But when his hands grew heavy and fell by his side then Amalek prevailed. The teaching is unmistakable. It is only as faith is exercised before God in the secret place of prayer, that faith will be triumphant in the continuous war that engages believers. "This is the victory that overcomes the world, even our faith" (1John 5:4). The Lord instructed Moses not only to record the event, but also to rehearse it in the ears of Joshua. This was important, for Joshua had to be made aware of the fact that the victory was the Lord's.

These exhortations are particularly needful at the beginning of the twenty first century. In western society, which we know best, the enemy has become noticeably very bold, and is becoming increasingly assertive. The Christian testimony is no longer tolerated as it used to be. Moral standards have fallen so dramatically, that sinners will now openly glory in their shame. It has also become clear that when issues of public interest are being discussed, the media are less inclined to involve anyone in the debate who will present a Biblical viewpoint.

Deeper grows the darkness round us,
Fiercer grows the strife.

Prayer - Personal & Corporate

It is an interesting detail, that since Moses hands tended to grow heavy, he was joined by two friends, Aaron and Hur. Their task was to support his hands until the going down of the sun. Moses, standing alone, might be thought of in terms of a believer engaged in personal prayer. This, of course, is a vital exercise and one that will carry its own reward. But those who engage in it most, know best how quickly weariness can set in. When Moses was joined by the others, it meant that two or three were now engaged in the same exercise. In this we have a fine picture of corporate prayer. We often sing:

"O the pure delight of a single hour,
That before thy throne I spend,
When I kneel in prayer and with thee, my God,
I commune as friend with friend."

Yet, if the truth were told, we may very well be singing beyond our experience if we are using these words in the context of private prayer. But if we put them in the context of corporate prayer, then we can sing them with real meaning. How often we have gathered with other believers to pray and our spirits have been raised and our souls revived. Coming to the prayer meeting, perhaps feeling discouraged and defeated, we have brought away with us time and again, a new understanding of the importance of corporate prayer.

Chapter 7
The Law and the Sanctuary

Judah was His sanctuary, and Israel His dominion. Psa.114:2.

Moses' father-in-law

After the victory over Amalek there was a brief interlude in the journey. During this interlude, Moses' father-in-law came from Midian and paid a brief visit to the camp. "And Moses told Jethro his father-in-law all that the Lord had done unto Pharaoh and to the Egyptians for Israel's sake ... and how the Lord delivered them. And Jethro rejoiced for all the goodness which the Lord had done to Israel ... And Jethro said, Blessed be the Lord, who has delivered you out of the hand of the Egyptians ... now I know that the Lord is greater than all gods" (Ex.18:8-11).

Although Moses entreated him to join them in their journey, Jethro was personally outside of all these things. The final word about him is that he went his way into his own land. In like manner, there are many within Christendom today who, like Jethro, both hear and know, and then go their own way, not willing to cast in their lot with the people of God. They are like Esau, that profane person, who lightly cast aside his birthright and afterward found no place of repentance, though he sought it with tears. (See Hebs.12:16,17.) Esau and Jethro appear to have been cast in the same mould.

Two Evidences of Faith

Israel's next move brought them to Sinai where they received the law and built the tabernacle. The people were reminded of how God had dealt with them and how, on the basis of redemption, He had brought them to Himself. "You have seen what I did to the

Egyptians, and how I bore you on eagles' wings and brought you to myself" (Ex.19:4). The ten statements of the moral law were also made at that time.

It should be emphasised that God did not give them the law while they were still in the house of bondage. Nor did He bargain with them and say, if you will do these things then I will deliver you. On the contrary, He dealt with them in pure grace. Their redemption was not conditioned on their own efforts, but now as redeemed ones, the Lord asked for their obedience.

The law was written with the finger of God, and it was holy, just and good. The people responded immediately and said, "All that the Lord has spoken we will do" (Ex.19:8). While their response may have been sincere, it completely underestimated their own propensity towards sin and wrong. Even before Moses came down from the mount, they had broken the very law they had pledged to maintain. They had violated the law in both its first and second statements and thus they were guilty of all. Happily the moral law was followed by the ceremonial law which revealed how such failure could be dealt with.

The House of God

Judging by their celebration song at the Red Sea, Israel's first thought after their deliverance, was of a house for the Lord. "The Lord is my strength and song, and He is become my salvation; He is my God, and I will prepare Him an habitation" (Ex.15:2). The thought itself was of God and it now found its visible expression in the tabernacle. Moses was reminded repeatedly to make the tabernacle according to the pattern that he had seen on the mount. And when it was completed and set up, it was done "according to all that the Lord commanded [Moses]." (See Ex.40:16.)

A Passover Hymn

The ideas behind both the law and the tabernacle are enshrined in one of the 'Hallel' psalms, or hymns of praise, which are still sung at Passover. Before the passover meal the people sing, "When Israel went out of Egypt, the house of Jacob from a people of strange language, Judah was His sanctuary, and Israel His dominion" (Psa.114:1,2). His sanctuary called for their worship and His dominion required their obedience. In a word, they were to be a people who, of their own voluntary will, would obey and serve the Lord.

These are the features the Lord still looks for in all who name His name. In many fellowships today new Christians are viewed simply as potential workers, but that is not how God views them. He sees them first of all as worshippers. As they worship the God of their salvation, they will discover the service they should render. Such service will then be from the heart; it will be rendered in obedience to God's will and to His glory.

The Priesthood

Since the tabernacle worship was a sacrifical system, the people were also given details of the priesthood, and of its attendant offerings. And it was here, at Sinai, that they were instructed in the various uses and services those ordinances were designed to fulfil.

Throughout the remainder of the wilderness period the tabernacle was pitched wherever the people camped. When they eventually entered the land it was pitched at Shiloh, and it remained there, until it was superseded by Solomon's magnificent temple in Jerusalem.

The tabernacle was Israel's house of God. It was to Israel what the local church is to believers today. Both the law and the tabernacle revealed at Sinai therefore, were deeply significant for Israel, and their relation to each other makes them impressively meaningful for us as well.

The Golden Calf

While they were still in the plains of Sinai the people displayed, in a very striking way, their innate capacity for idolatry. They devised a god of their own. They set up a golden calf and worshipped it in place of Jehovah. They said, "These are your gods, O Israel, which brought you up out of the land of Egypt" (Ex.32:4). Many have debated Aaron's involvement in this incident, some accusing him and others excusing him. One thing is clear, Aaron's weakness at this point made it easier for the people to behave as they did.

Ostensibly, the reason for their unseemly conduct was Moses' delay in coming down from the mount, but the true reason was that they had turned away in heart from the Lord. In this incident there is much for us to learn because we too have found that "the heart is deceitful above all things, and desperately wicked; who can know it?" (Jer.17:9)

The words of the law had been read and they had committed themselves without reserve to obey them. Their commitment had even been established in a covenant sealed in sacrifical blood. And then came this terrible offence which brought upon their heads the full weight of the broken law.

Around three thousand men perished that day and the Lord threatened to withdraw His presence from the congregation. He would still drive out the enemy and give them the land on the basis of the promise He had made to their fathers, but now He would be content simply to send an angel before them.

Advocacy of Moses

But Moses could not accept such a state of affairs. However much he had the land before him, Moses prized even more the presence of the Lord with His people. Now, and not for the only time in this incredible journey, we find him pleading Israel's cause as their advocate with God. He said, "If your presence go not with me, carry us not up from here" (Ex.33:15). The Lord graciously heard his cry and renewed to him the assurance of His presence. "He said, My presence shall go with you, and I will give you rest." (See Ex.33:14.) In this sweet assurance Moses and his people would soon leave Sinai and proceed to the next stage of their pilgrimage.

A consciousness of His presence with them in the onward march of life is what God's people have always coveted above everything else. In a letter to one of his parishioners, from his prison in Aberdeen, Samuel Rutherford wrote, 'Jesus Christ came into my cell last night, and every stone in it glowed like a ruby.' To make Moses' prayer our own would be an appropriate way for us to begin each day, "If your presence go not with us, carry us not up from here."

When the storms of life are raging,
Stand by me.
When the world is tossing me
Like a ship upon the sea,
Thou who rulest wind and water,
Stand by me.

Sinai is probably the best point at which to ascribe nationhood to Israel. From Sinai onward they had their own legal system and were therefore in a position to govern themselves. But their law was God's law. It was given to them as a redeemed people to obey God. And in the same way the sanctuary, or tabernacle, was given to them that they might worship God, the God who had fulfilled His covenant in delivering them from Egypt. The considerable time spent at Sinai had not been wasted. The people were now better equipped for their onward march to Canaan.

Stage Three
The Spiritual Mind and the Carnal mind
(From Sinai to Kadesh Barnea)

Chapter 8

Marching On

To be spiritually minded is life and peace.
Rom.8:6.

About two years had been spent at Sinai and the time had now come for the people to move on. The third stage of their journey beckoned, the stage that would bring them to the wilderness of Paran, which was just south of Canaan and due west of Edom. It would be from Paran, and specifically from Kadesh Barnea, that the people would send men to spy out the land.

The total journey from Sinai to the promised land should have taken about eleven days. (See Deut.1:2,3.) In the event, it stretched out to some thirty eight years. The reason for that excessive delay is the story of this eventful third leg of the journey. In our last section we noted that the prominent feature in their journey from the Red Sea to Sinai was the importance of faith. But now the emphasis is on the spiritual condition of the people themselves.

Spiritual Conditions

In every age certain moral and spiritual conditions have been necessary for the cultivation and exercise of faith. Those conditions were present to some degree as the people set out on the third stage of the journey. Alas, they were soon to be tragically dissipated. When they left Sinai the people might reasonably be described as a spiritually minded people. But before long they were seized by a mean and capricious spirit, that completely undermined their spiritual condition.

Hitherto the congregation has been before us, by and large, by way of example and pattern, but now they come before us by way of the most solemn warning. This part of the journey presents us with a striking illustration of Paul's doctrine, "To be carnally minded is death, but to be spiritually minded is life and peace" (Rom.8:6).

The believers at Galatia were severely reprimanded by the same apostle, for succumbing to the same kind of spirit. "O foolish Galatians, who has bewitched you, that you should not obey the truth ... Are you so foolish? Having begun in the Spirit, are you now made perfect by the flesh?" (Gal.3:1-3) The Galatian warning is graphically illustrated in what happened between Sinai and Paran. Let us take careful note and beware, always having in mind that these things are recorded for our instruction.

The Pillar of Cloud

While at Sinai two things had been clearly established for their guidance. From the beginning, the pillar of cloud by day and of fire by night, was the visible symbol of God's presence with them. But at this point the pillar seems to have taken on a new and added significance. Its movement would now determine their length of stay in any given location. From that point forward, when the cloud moved they would move, when the cloud stopped they would stop, and while the cloud lingered they would tarry.

The pillar of cloud is said to have occupied three different positions in relation to the camp. Sometimes it went before to guide them. At other times it stood behind to guard them. And then at times it hovered over the camp to govern them. This meant that all their movements, throughout the entire journey, were governed by the pillar of cloud and of fire.

This marvellous provision took away from the people any responsibility about when or where they should move. It meant that they were never left to their own devices. All that was required of them was a simple and candid obedience. In this way God provided much needed direction for His people. As a pilgrim people they certainly stood in need of such guidance, for they trod an uncertain path through a wild and trackless wilderness.

An Unerring Guide

We too need an unerring guide, for our path is no more certain than theirs. The Holy Spirit is given specifically to believers to guide them into all truth and to lead them in right paths. Evidently there is a parallel to be drawn between the cloud and the Spirit. Of those wilderness days Paul wrote, "They were all baptised unto Moses in the cloud and in the sea" (1Cor.10:2). And of our own day he went on to say, "By one Spirit were we all baptised into one body" (1Cor.12:13).

Having received the gift of the Spirit, we are now to be led by the Spirit. "For as many as are led by the Spirit of God, they are the sons of God" (Rom.8:14). In this respect the Lord Jesus is our perfect exemplar, for as He passed through this world, it is recorded of Him that He too was led by the Spirit. "And Jesus ... was led by the Spirit into the wilderness" (Luke 4:1).

The pillar of cloud and of fire accompanied the children of Israel from the first day of their journey. In the same way, from the beginning of our Christian experience we have the presence of the indwelling Holy Spirit. Moreover, just as the cloud remained with them all the way through until they entered Canaan, so the Saviour promised that the Holy Spirit will abide with us forever. (See John 14:16.) However lonely we may feel at times, we are never alone in the journey of faith.

The Silver Trumpets

In addition to being guided by the pillar of cloud and of fire, they were also guided by the silver trumpets. (See Num.10:1-10.) Stress is laid upon the fact that while there were two trumpets, there was just one instrument. "Make thee two trumpets of silver; of a whole piece shalt thou make them." It is not difficult to see in the silver trumpets striking images of the written word of God. We have only one Bible, but it is given to us in two Testaments. We must value it as a whole and we must learn to distinguish between its parts.

While the trumpets were used at other times, their main purpose was to arouse the camp. A certain note would indicate when the whole assembly was to be gathered. A different note would indicate when the journey was to be resumed. The priests sounded the trumpets, and the people were instructed to keep their ears attuned and be able to distinguish between the various sounds. In this way all their meetings and marchings were regulated by the silver trumpets.

In the same way we must listen to the Lord as He speaks to us through His word. The entire book is there for our guidance and as we ponder its pages; phrases and sentences, and sometimes whole verses will stand out before us. They will strike us like the different notes from the silver trumpets. In this way, the Lord, through His word, will direct our paths. And we should constantly avail ourselves of this wonderful provision. The psalmist surely spoke for us all when he said, "Thy word is a lamp unto my feet, and a light unto my path" (Psa.119:105).

The Journey Resumed

It was surely a marvellous spectacle when the people set out from Sinai to come to the wilderness of Paran. The sound of the silver trumpets would have been heard, loud and clear. And then, with standards unfurled, the entire camp would be on the move, always careful to follow the pillar of cloud going on before. They moved in a precise and orderly fashion. "In the first place went the standard of the camp of the children of Judah according to their armies ... And the standard of the camp of Reuben set forward according to their armies ... " (See Num.10:14,18.)

The account tells us, "At the commandment of the Lord they rested in the tents, and at the commandment of the Lord they journeyed:

they kept the charge of the Lord, at the commandment of the Lord by the hand of Moses" (Num.9:23). Many centuries later, their New Testament counterparts were the believers who formed the church at Colosse in Asia Minor. To them Paul wrote, "For though I am absent in the flesh, yet am I with you in the spirit, joying and beholding your order, and the stedfastness of your faith in Christ" (Col.2:5).

Clearly it is with some confidence we are able to say, that at the time of their departure from Sinai, the children of Israel were a reasonably spiritually minded people. But this was soon to change. And had we been speaking to them a little later, we might well have used the words of another and said, "You did run well; who did hinder you that you should not obey the truth?" (Gal. 5:7).

Chapter 9

An Ominous Change

To be carnally minded is death. Rom.8:6.

Somewhere between Sinai and Paran, a sense of foreboding took possession of the whole congregation. Another spirit, a spirit that was not of God, seized their minds. It was a spirit alien to a redeemed people. We read that, "when the people complained, it displeased the Lord" (Num.11:1). The marginal rendering is much stronger, "the people were as it were complainers." Complaining had become a way of life.

A Complaining Spirit

This negative and carnal spirit had both fruit and root. Its fruit was noxious and virulent in the extreme, and its pernicious outcome profoundly affected the whole company. Tragically, it even impacted on the God-appointed leaders. Moreover, it led to the heavenly manna being despised, and it became the primary cause behind the failure of that entire generation to enter their promised land.

As to its root, the first symptoms were manifested at the Red Sea. When the people saw the Egyptians pursuing them they cried out in fear. "And they said unto Moses, Because there were no graves in Egypt, have you taken us away to die in the wilderness? ... It had been better for us to serve the Egyptians, than that we should die in the wilderness" (Ex.14:11,12). There was a further manifestation of this evil principle when they came to Marah. Because the waters of Marah were bitter, they murmured against Moses. (See Ex.15:23,24.)

In the following chapter they murmured again, but now it was against Moses and Aaron. At that point Moses sounded a note of caution, he said, "the Lord hears your murmurings which you murmur against Him: and what are we? Your murmurings are not against us, but against the Lord" (Ex.16:8). But things did not improve and in the next chapter we find them at it still. This time they went even further, "They tempted the Lord, saying, Is the Lord among us or not?" (Ex.17:7)

Their whole experience, including the very position they now occupied, cried out that God was with them. Had it not been so, they would still have been groaning in the house of bondage. At the beginning of the journey it must have seemed unthinkable that they should have murmured as they did. Yet experience shows that things are not much different today, for when some difficulty presses itself on us, our reactions are often quite similar to theirs. We, too, are tempted to doubt the Lord's presence with us. Sometimes we might even wonder if He ever had been with us. In such circumstances we too can easily succumb to the same spirit of complaining.

Thankfulness

Paul warned that an unthankful spirit would be a prominent feature of the last days, and for this reason he exhorted believers to cultivate a spirit of thanksgiving. We are to make the Lord Jesus our pattern. We read of Him giving thanks on a number of very significant occasions. And what gave special character to those thanksgivings was that they were all in the context of negative circumstances.

Take, for example, the occasion of His rejection by Capernaum, and the cities in which most of His mighty works were done. "At that time Jesus answered and said, I thank thee, O Father, Lord of heaven and earth ... " (Matt.11:25). And on the eve of His arraignment before Pilate and His subsequent crucifixion, "He took bread, and gave thanks ... " (Luke 22:19). In the background of all these references we seem to hear Him say, "I have given you an example, that you should do as I have done ... " (John 13:15).

The persistent whimpering of the people throughout the journey must have given the Lord many occasions to abandon them, but that is not His way. Instead, He furnished them a table in the wilderness, and man did eat angels' food. He slaked their thirst with water from the smitten rock. "He brought streams also out of the rock, and caused waters to run down like rivers" (Psa.78:16).

A Chronic Condition

But the carnal spirit had become endemic, and each time of testing brought it to the surface. This, of course, gave them opportunity to judge it. But instead of judging it, they nurtured it, they kept it warm until the next time. It is really quite palpable that their murmurings usually arose over the minor and everyday things of life. They had seen God meet their need in the big things, such as the dividing of the Red Sea and the overthrow of Pharaoh's armies, but they could not trust Him for the little things.

With true insight it has been said that it is not so much the greatness of our troubles as the littleness of our spirit that causes us to complain. We must purge ourselves of whatever negative impulse may arise within us in times of testing, for that is the thing that is hindering, and may even stifle, the work of sanctification in our souls. God uses the testing times to reveal to us the things we need to judge, and these are usually things we might otherwise overlook or excuse.

Moreover, we should never forget the exhortation which says, "My son, despise not the chastening of the Lord, nor faint when you are rebuked of Him; for whom the Lord loves He chastens ... and no chastening for the present seems to be joyous, but grievous; nevertheless, afterward it yields the peaceable fruit of righteousness to them who are exercised by it" (Hebs.12: 5-11).

Somewhere along the Paran road, what had long simmered among the people, boiled over. The infection had not been treated, and it became a chronic condition. The end result was to prove far reaching indeed. We are told of both David and Solomon that their last days were not up to the standard of their first days. And it was the same with the believers at Ephesus. The Lord's lament over them was this, "You have left your first love" (Rev.2:4). William Cowper understood these things well when he wrote:

Where is the blessedness I knew,
When first I saw the Lord?
Where is the soul-refreshing view
Of Jesus and His word?

We have yet to see how this carnal condition led to the most bitter recrimination between the people and their leaders, and even between the leaders themselves. And we are to learn how it issued in that whole generation perishing in the wilderness, when they might have entered into the land and enjoyed the good things God had in store for them. We must all beware!

Chapter 10
The Mixed Multitude

A mixed multitude went up also with them.
Ex.12:38.

The effects of this carnal, fractious spirit were immediate as well as long term. An oppressive aggravation gripped the people and this in turn allowed the mixed multitude enough space to assert themselves. The mixed multitude were people who had witnessed the power of God displayed on Israel's behalf in Egypt. Although they had never been 'under the blood' themselves, they had decided to cast in their lot with the redeemed of the Lord. It may even be that in some instances their motivation had been inter-marriage.

Whatever the reason, although they were with Israel, they were not of Israel. They were not a part of the theocracy; they were not true hearted Israelites. But the mixed multitude had crossed the sea, and they had now companied with Israel these two years. Yet their hearts were still in Egypt, and their desires after the things of Egypt remained unchanged. And now, at this critical moment, we read, "the mixed multitude that was among them fell to lusting ... and said, Who shall give us flesh to eat?" (Num.11:4).

Christendom

However innocent it may have appeared at the first, the presence of these people in the camp was a constant irritant. Their presence doubtless added to the numbers, but numbers are not always a blessing. Gideon found it better to have three hundred men, loyal and true, than to have thirty two thousand whose hearts were divided.

Several of our Lord's parables anticipated that Christendom would be of a similar mixed composition. And the activity of the enemy has ensured that this has been so. A typical example of what we mean is seen in the parable of the ten virgins. (See Matt.25:1-13.) The virgins were so alike, while the bridegroom tarried it was impossible to tell the wise from the foolish. But when the bridegroom came all was made clear.

Christendom very soon became a mixed multitude, an unholy mixture of wheat and tares. And it remains to this day a sad amalgam of saved and unsaved, of those who are the Lord's and those who are not. It is easily possible to become identified with people who are truly the Lord's without having a heart identification with the Lord Himself. Indeed, it is fairly evident that the activity and influence of a mixed multitude in her midst, is very seriously weakening the Church's present testimony. Better to have two or three who truly love the Lord than a large number who attach themselves for other and lesser reasons.

It was with a heavy heart that Paul warned the Ephesian elders of this same problem. "For I know this, that after my departing shall grievous wolves enter in among you, not sparing the flock. Also of your own selves shall men arise, speaking perverse things, to draw away disciples after them" (Acts 20:29,30).

Onions and Garlic

The capriciousness of the people as they approached Paran gave the mixed multitude the opportunity they needed to express their pent up fustrations. This, in turn, added to the general sense of aggravation, and before long it spread throughout the whole congregation. "And the children of Israel also wept again, and said, Who shall give us flesh to eat? We remember the fish which we did eat in Egypt freely; the cucumbers, and the melons, and the leeks, and the onions, and the garlic. But now our soul is dried away; and there is nothing at all, beside this manna, before our eyes" (Num.11:4-6).

Some will want to argue about these things. They will ask, what was so wrong with the onions and garlic of Egypt? The short answer is that in themselves there was probably nothing wrong with them. But the fact remains that the lusting for these things took away the people's appetite for the divinely provided food, and even led to the manna being despised. And therein lay their danger.

What a sad spectacle all this presents, the redeemed people openly preferring the food of Egypt to the bread of Heaven. We have already seen how the manna speaks of the Lord Jesus. It follows therefore, that whatever reduces our appreciation of Him is not for us. We must ask, even of apparently innocent things, do they cause us to think less of the Saviour? If that is so, then let us refrain from them.

It scarcely needs to be pointed out that in this frame of mind the people quite forgot the cruel bondage they had suffered when in Egypt. At a later date, Moses would impress this on their minds, "You shall remember that you were a bondman in the land of Egypt, and the Lord your God redeemed you" (Deut.15:15). For our part, shall we forget "the rock from which [we] are hewn, and the hole of the pit from which [we] are digged?" (Isa.51:1)

He Gave them their Request

In spite of their intransigence the Lord miraculously provided flesh for the people to eat. Even Moses doubted how this could be done. He said, "The people, among whom I am are six hundred thousand footmen; and thou hast said, I will give them flesh, that they may eat a whole month. Shall the flocks and the herds be slain for them, to suffice them? or shall all the fish of the sea be gathered for them, to suffice them?" (Num.11:21,22) There was a mild rebuke in the Lord's reply. He simply asked Moses, "Is the Lord's hand become short?"

The history tells us how this was actually achieved. "There went forth a wind from the Lord, and brought quails from the sea, and let them fall by the camp, as it were a day's journey on this side, and as it were a day's journey on the other side, round about the camp, and as it were two cubits high upon the face of the earth. And the people stood up all that day, and all that night, and all the next day, and they gathered the quails" (Num.11:31,32).

But all was at a price. The rather terse comment of the psalmist on this event calls for reflection. "He gave them their request, but sent leanness into their soul" (Psa.106:15). They forfeited the spiritual mind that had marked them when they left Sinai, and not until that whole generation had passed away, did the people recover from the leanness of soul that afflicted them at this time.

Chapter 11
A Spirit of Jealousy

Jealousy is cruel as the grave.
Song of S. 8:6.

The disaffection of the children of Israel also profoundly impacted their leaders. Even Moses found himself under reproach from persons of no less stature than Miriam and Aaron. "And Miriam and Aaron spoke against Moses because of the Ethiopian woman whom he had married" (Num.12:1). The order of the names here must be significant, Miriam first and then Aaron. The garden of Eden was about to be revisited. Clearly there was a double failure on this occasion as there had been in the garden. Aaron, like Adam, was not exercising his authority, and Miriam, like Eve, was usurping her place.

Moses' marriage was only a pretext, since who he married was his own business. Had they been as forward in judging themselves as they were in judging their brother, this whole matter might have been contained. Paul said, "If we would judge ourselves we should not be judged" (1Cor.11:31). He meant quite simply that where there is true self-judgement, no other judgement is necessary. In the case of Miriam and Aaron, the Lord stepped in to judge because they had failed to judge themselves.

Jealousy

That the real motive behind this attack on Moses was jealousy, became immediately plain when they said, "Has the Lord indeed spoken only by Moses? Has He not spoken also by us?" (Num.12:2) They clearly wanted Moses to share his authority with them to a greater degree. They may even have wanted the freedom to act independently of Moses. The incident certainly illustrates a very practical truth. Where there is some hidden evil in the inward parts, and that evil remains unjudged, it will eventually come out into the open.

We are told, somewhat portentously, "The Lord heard it" (Num.12:2). Added to that we read, "The Lord spoke suddenly unto Moses, and unto Aaron, and unto Miriam. Come out you three unto the tabernacle of the congregation. And they three came out" (Num.12:4). In this way the Lord isolated the problem so that He might deal with it more effectively.

We will not stop to discuss the commendations the Lord paid to His servant Moses at this time, but they do need to be recognised. The Lord said He would speak to others through dreams and visions, but not so with Moses. To him He would speak face to face, and plainly, rather than in dark sayings. He described Moses as being faithful in all His house. The context says that "Moses was very meek, above all the men who were upon the face of the earth" (Num.12:3). Meekness is a spirit that does not seek revenge and this was the thing that shone through in Moses' reactions at this time.

It is a great pity that Miriam and Aaron did not give due credence to these things. Yet we must ask again, has anything changed over the years? All who engage in congregational work know how easily people can find fault, even when there is much to commend. This inclination comes easily, it is a trait common to humankind. Therein, of course, lies the rub. It is natural, but it is not spiritual, and it is so unlike the Lord Jesus. What penetrating judgements He rightly passed on the churches of Asia Minor. Yet in almost every instance, He first found something to praise. (See Rev.2&3.) What a wonderful Saviour He is, and how sad it is that the saved are often so unlike Him.

Divine Discipline

Having separated the three from the congregation, the Lord then parted Aaron and Miriam from Moses. After that He proceeded to address them in tones that were at once severe and majestic. When He had finished speaking, Miriam stood alone, a leper as white as snow. Miriam had allowed herself to be caught up in the unwholesome spirit that was so rampant in the camp at the time, and in the end she had become a casualty of it.

Aaron entreated Moses on her behalf, and Moses interceded for her. And once again the Lord showed Himself a God ready to pardon. Miriam was eventually healed, but two things should be noted. She was shut out from the congregation for seven days. This must have been a severe punishment for one who was held in such high honour.

After all, when she was still a girl, Miriam had played an important part in the salvation of Moses. And it was Miriam who had led the praises of the women, when the entire congregation of Israel celebrated their deliverance from Pharaoh at the Red Sea. But having signally failed to judge herself, she came under the judgement of the Lord.

At a Standstill

The other thing to note is this, "The people journeyed not till Miriam was brought in again" (Num.12:15). This meant that the operation of the carnal spirit, especially among the leaders, had the additional effect of bringing to a standstill the congregation as a whole. The same scenario was repeated some years later when Achan sinned at Jericho.

Both incidents should bring home to us the possible effect on the whole, of sin in one member of the fellowship. Let all who have responsibility for leadership take note, and let the rest of us beware, lest a seed of jealousy should be allowed to take root in our own hearts. For "jealousy is cruel as the grave; its coals are coals of

Stage Four
The Years of Wandering
(From Kadesh and back to Kadesh)

Chapter 12

Kadesh Barnea

An evil heart of unbelief.
Hebs. 3:12.

After the debacle described in our last chapter the people moved on and finally came to the wilderness of Paran. They encamped at Kadesh Barnea which became a profoundly significant place for Israel. Kadesh became a watershed in every sense of the term. It is a name written in flaming letters, for Kadesh proved a turning point in the entire enterprise so far as that whole generation was concerned.

Before Kadesh the children of Israel were pilgrims advancing with purpose at the commandment of the Lord. After Kadesh they were simply wanderers going round in circles in the wilderness. They were like the proverbial door on its hinges, all the time moving backwards and forwards, but never getting anywhere.

This state of affairs continued for thirty-eight years, until that generation had passed away. It was only when they had come full circle and were brought back again to Kadesh, that God moved to bring the new or second generation of the people into the land of Canaan by the hand of Joshua. (See Numbers 20.)

Sometimes Kadesh is linked with the wilderness of Paran, and sometimes with the wilderness of Zin. The reason for this seems to be that Kadesh straddled the border between the two areas, a border which at best was probably ill-defined. But its chief significance lay in the fact that Kadesh was the gateway to Canaan. And it was from there they sent the twelve men to spy out the land.

In spite of the undisciplined temper of the people when they arrived at Kadesh, the word from the Lord remained unchanged. An unconditional covenant had been made with Abraham; and the God who made it, would be true to His word. Hence His command to this gainsaying people. "Behold, I have set the land before you; go in and possess the land which the Lord swore unto your fathers, Abraham, Isaac, and Jacob, to give unto them and to their seed after them" (Deut.1:8).

The Day of Temptation

The story of Kadesh begins with these words. "And the Lord spoke unto Moses, saying, Send thou men, that they may search the land of Canaan ... of every tribe of their fathers shall you send a man, every one a ruler among them" (Num.13:1,2.). But this command must be read in the context of Deuteronomy chapter one. For while the book of Numbers gives the public history of the people, Deuteronomy takes us behind the scenes and gives us their private history.

Even before the people left Sinai, Moses had restated the basis on which they could proceed to the land. He later reminded them of this when he said, "I commanded you at that time all the things which you should do" (Deut.1:18). For their part, all that was required was obedience to the commandment of the Lord by the hand of Moses. And now, upon their arrival at Kadesh, Moses said, "You are come unto the mountain of the Amorites, which the Lord our God doth give unto us. Behold, the Lord your God has set the land before you. Go up and possess it" (Deut.1:20,21).

Sending the Spies

Then the people came to Moses and said, "We will send men before us, and they shall search out the land, and bring us word again by what way we must go up, and into what cities we shall come." Sending the spies, therefore, was an idea that appears to have originated with the people. Moses' record of the incident reads, "You came near unto me, every one of you, and said, We will send men before us." (See Deut.1:20-22.) The Lord seemingly condescended to their request and allowed the spies to be sent. And Moses too, probably in line with the Lord's response, went along with the idea.

There are several instances of this sort of thing in scripture. The Lord often seems to condescend to meet people in the state in which He finds them at a given time. We saw an instance of this when the people despised the manna and demanded flesh to eat. The Lord deigned to meet them in their poor spiritual condition at that time, and He gave them flesh to eat. (See comments on chapter 11.)

A later example of this same thing was when the people demanded a king. The Lord told Samuel to anoint Saul, but the experiment was a disaster. The idea of kingship was certainly in God's will, but the people could not wait God's time, when the true king would be revealed. Moreover, their motivation was all wrong for they said, "Make us a king to judge us like all the nations" (1Sam.8:5). And so it was at Kadesh when the people stood at the very gateway to the land.

Unbelief

In itself the sending of the spies may not have been so bad, had the motivation behind it been right. But an evil heart of unbelief lurked beneath the surface. Moses solemn charge was this, "In this thing you did not believe the Lord your God" (Deut.1:32). Evidently they felt they could have more confidence in the word of frail man than in the word of the living God. In any case, they would send men to satisify themselves that what God had said about the land was really true.

Underlying the epistle to the Hebrews is this simple question, "Why did that generation not enter the land?" The reply given agrees with Moses' own assessment and is quite candid, "they ... entered not in because of unbelief" (Hebs.4:6). The rather forthright comment of the psalmist was this, "They turned back and tempted God, and limited the Holy One of Israel" (Psa.78:41). This is probably the best definition of unbelief we can find anywhere in scripture. Unbelief is the sin of limiting God.

Kadesh Barnea proved a sombre day for the generation that came out of Egypt. It is called the day of temptation in the wilderness. (See Hebs.3:8.) Temptation always has at its heart a choice, and the choice is always the same. It is a choice between the revealed will of God on the one hand, and selfwill and unbelief on the other. That was the essential choice before the people at Kadesh. For our part, we are presently living in our day of temptation, and while our circumstances may be different, the principles of the case remain the same.

Caleb and Joshua

When the spies returned, the unbelief that lay behind their mission was compounded. The twelve were hopelessly divided. The same intelligence was known equally by all twelve, but two of their number interpreted it differently from the others. Caleb and Joshua, insisted that the people were well able to possess the land. The others brought an evil report which discouraged the whole company. Their majority report was factual enough but it had one very serious weakness, it left God out of the reckoning.

Caleb and Joshua saw what the others had seen and, they too, had tasted the fruit of the land. Moreover, they were equally aware of the difficulties of the task. The inhabitants were strong and the cities well fortified. But beyond all that, they also saw the Lord. They said, "If the Lord delight in us, then He will bring us into this land, and give it us" (Num.14:8). Thus they tried to still the frenetic temper of the people.

The others could only see themselves in comparison with the giants who occupied the land. And they openly declared themselves to be no match for the enemy. Their report devastated the people and the whole congregation became demoralised. The record tells us that when they heard it, "All the congregation lifted up their voice, and cried; and the people wept that night" (Num.14:1).

As a side effect, that negative report gave further opportunity for the old whimpering spirit to vent itself again. Once more, the people murmured against Moses and against Aaron. This time they even threatened to appoint a captain who would lead them back to Egypt.

Chapter 13

Grace and Government

I swore in my wrath, they shall not enter
into my rest. Hebs. 3:11.

It is a most significant thing that God never allowed the people He
had redeemed to return to Egypt. That would have cancelled out
their redemption and such a thing just could not be. In this, God
was acting in grace. But at Kadesh we see God acting in government
as well. Not allowed to go back to Egypt, they were not allowed to
go on to Canaan either. "The Lord spoke unto Moses and unto
Aaron, saying ... Say unto them ... Your carcasses shall fall in this
wilderness ... you shall not come into the land ... except Caleb, the
son of Jephunneh, and Joshua, the son of Nun" (Num.14: 26-30).

The Second Generation

Happily, that was not the end of the story for the Lord went on to
say, "When you are come into the land of your habitations ..."
(Num.15:2). This does not contradict His earlier statement, for the
reference here is to the second generation who in due time possessed
the land under Joshua. There had been great failure on the part of
the generation that came out of Egypt, but there was no failure
with God. The integrity of His promise would be maintained. And
the people, in their second generation, would eventually enter the
land which had been given to them for an everlasting possession.

This setting aside of the first generation in favour of the second, is
a striking instance of a constantly recurring biblical theme. We see
it in Cain and Abel, in Ishmael and Isaac, and in Esau and Jacob.
In each instance there was a definite setting aside of the firstborn
in favour of the second. In the wider picture, God has set aside the

first man, Adam, who failed, and He has taken up His purposes in a second man, a last Adam, the Lord from heaven, of whom the scriptures assert, "He shall not fail" (Isa.42:4).

The Meaning of Canaan

At this point we might pause to inquire into the spiritual meaning of the failure of that generation to enter the land, and to ask if it has any lesson for us today. Canaan is often referred to as representing heaven. But this can only be so in the rather limited sense that Canaan came at the end of the journey. Its real significance is much more immediate. Canaan represents God's full purpose for His people. He would not only bring Israel out of Egypt, and through the desert, He would also bring them into Canaan.

His ultimate intention was that this people, in their own land, should fulfil His will and be a testimony to the nations. They would be a witness against idolatry, and an example to the nations of the blessedness of a people whose God is the Lord. At Sinai the Lord had spelt this out, "You have seen what I did unto the Egyptians, and how I bore you on eagles' wings and brought you unto myself. Now therefore, if you will obey my voice indeed, and keep my covenant, then you shall be a peculiar treasure unto me above all people; for all the earth is mine: And you shall be unto me a kingdom of priests, and an holy nation" (Ex.19:4-6).

The Will of God

In the same way, God has more in mind for us than that our salvation should simply be a kind of escape from perdition. His purpose in saving me, said Paul, was "to reveal His Son in me" (Gal.1:16). The same apostle declared in another place, "Whom He did foreknow, He also did predestinate to be conformed to the image of His Son, that He might be the firstborn among many brethren" (Rom.8:29).

This means that there can be no finality to Christian experience in this life. On the contrary, there is a constant pressing on towards spiritual maturity, "Till we all come in the unity of the faith, and of the knowledge of the Son of God, unto a perfect man, unto the measure of the stature of the fullness of Christ" (Eph.4:13). '

In a day when gospel preaching places great emphasis on decisions and on numbers, it is good to keep before us the apostolic goal. "... warning every man, and teaching every man in all wisdom, that we may present every man perfect |mature| in Christ Jesus. For this I also labour, striving according to His working, who works in me mightily" (Col.1:28,29).

The spiritual equivalent to that generation missing the land, therefore, is not that present day believers may miss heaven at the last. Rather, it is the very real possibility of missing the full purpose of our calling in the present; of failing to realise in the here and now, that good and acceptable and perfect will of God. Conversely, those believers who seek to stand "perfect and complete in all the will of God" have their counterpart in the second generation who entered Canaan.

It is to be feared that many today have come a certain distance in divine things, only to vegetate in a kind of spiritual vacuum. They have become like a stagnant pool, rather than the watered garden they were intended to be. The generation that perished in the wilderness carries a solemn warning for us all. Let us resolve, in dependence on the Holy Spirit, that we shall not stop short of all the will of God for our lives.

An Advocate with God

A relieving factor in this rather depressing narrative is the role that Moses played. Here we see him as the intercessor and advocate of his people. It is interesting to trace the many occasions when Moses fulfilled this role. We had a notable instance of it, when the people danced before the golden calf at Sinai. And also at the time of Miriam's leprosy just before they came to Kadesh. Aaron entreated Moses on her behalf and he, in turn, interceded for her before the Lord.

Now at Kadesh, "the Lord said unto Moses ... I will smite them with the pestilence, and disinherit them, and will make of you a greater nation and mightier than they." But Moses' reply was outstanding, he renounced all self-interest and said, "Then the Egyptians shall hear it ... and they will tell it to the inhabitants of this land; for they have heard, Lord, that you are among this people." He then went on to plead their cause. "Pardon, I beseech you, the iniquity of this people according unto the greatness of your mercy, and as you have forgiven this people, from Egypt even until now. And the Lord said, I have pardoned according to your word." (See Num.14: 11-20.)

But we must not pass too quickly over the impact that Kadesh-Barnea had on Moses personally. At the time, he noted in his diary: "I fell down before the Lord forty days and forty nights ... because the Lord had said He would destroy you, I prayed, therefore, unto the Lord, and said, O Lord God, destroy not your people and your inheritance, whom you have redeemed ... lest the land from which you brought us out say, Because the Lord was not able to bring them into the land which He promised them, and because He hated them, He has brought them out to slay them in the wilderness" (Deut.9: 25-28).

In all these instances Moses speaks powerfully of the Lord Jesus who is our Intercessor in heaven. Scripture asserts of Him that "He is able also to save them to the uttermost that come unto God by Him, seeing He ever lives to make intercession for them" (Hebs.7:25). Our Advocate with God is not some mere man, be he priest or prelate, but the Lord Jesus Christ Himself. The apostle John wrote, "My little children, these things write I unto you, that you sin not. And if any man sin, we have an advocate with the Father, Jesus Christ the righteous" (1John 2:1).

Chapter 14

No Longer Pilgrims

Return, you backsliding children, and I will heal
your backslidings. Jer. 3:22.

The tragedy of Kadesh resulted in the pilgrimage being interrupted,
and it was not resumed for thirty-eight years. So the camp turned
away from the land of promise and turned back towards the
wilderness by way of the Red Sea. Some considerable time was
spent in the region of Mount Seir, and in the plains of Moab and in
other places. But the people had now become wanderers in the
great wilderness. They were simply going round in circles, until
eventually, the command was given to turn northwards and they
were brought back again to Kadesh.

It is helpful to combine the period before they first came to Kadesh,
and the period after they returned to Kadesh thirty-eight years later,
and then to distinguish between those two periods and the period
of wandering that lay between. The wilderness journey itself, apart
from that long and fretful interval, was God's will for His people.
But the long and trying interval lay outside of His will for them.

A Rebellious Spirit

During those intervening years the carnal condition of the people
expressed itself in open rebellion against Moses and Aaron. Perhaps
the most notable instance of this was when Korah, Dathan and
Abiram, took men and rose up before Moses. "They gathered
themselves together against Moses and against Aaron, and said
unto them, You take too much upon you, seeing all the congregation
all holy, every one of them, and the Lord is among them: wherefore,

then, lift you up yourselves above the congregation of the Lord?"
(Num.16:3)

The rebellion was well orchestrated and skilfully managed, and
the whole matter was cogently argued. It was designed to have the
widest possible popular appeal. Ostensibly, it was an appeal for
more democracy, and for equality of opportunity, in the affairs of
the camp. The argument was simple: all the congregation is holy.
But in reality, it was a bold challenge to the Lord's authority, at
whose divine appointment, Moses and Aaron held their positions.
It would appear that the largely unsuspecting people were swept
along in the politics of the occasion.

Democracy and Theocracy

There is an important difference between democracy and theocracy.
The former is where everyone may cast an opinion into the debate
in the hope that a majority opinion will emerge. That is political
democracy. But theocracy is where the people of God gather
together in subjection to the Lordship of Christ, and in dependence
upon the Holy Spirit, to wait upon the Lord to reveal His mind. No
one person has a monopoly on the mind of the Lord, but when His
people meet after this fashion, a consensus will usually emerge
which might fairly be taken as representing the Lord's mind on a
given issue. That consensus, if it is of God, will always accord
with the teaching of His word.

Great care, however, must be taken at this point. For in countries
where the political model is a democracy of one kind or another,
there is a very natural tendency for believers to simply transfer the
democracy of their political parties to the affairs of the house of
God. This must inevitably lead to calamity, for we finish up with
an unacceptable intrusion of the natural mind into spiritual things.
We should never forget that it was by wisdom, and not by ignorance,
that the world failed to recognise our Lord Jesus Christ. (See
1Cor.2:8.) By all means, let us apply our best minds to the work of
the Lord, but let us also insist that those minds themselves are
subject to His will.

The Judgement of Korah

The point at which this confrontation with Korah is introduced, suggests that rebellion was the characteristic attitude of the people during the period of the wandering. It was certainly a daring challenge to the authority of Moses and Aaron. Together those two great men present us with a double type of our Lord Jesus Christ. "Wherefore, holy brethren, partakers of the heavenly calling, consider the Apostle [Moses] and High Priest [Aaron] of our profession, Christ Jesus" (Hebs.3:1). The challenge of Korah and his people, therefore, raises for us the whole question of our subjection to the Lordship of Christ.

The reaction of the two leaders was quite magnificent. "When Moses heard it, he fell on his face. And he spoke unto Korah and unto all his company, saying, Even tomorrow the Lord will show who are His, and who is holy" (Num.16:4,5). The chapter goes on to show how God vindicated Moses. Korah and his people were told to take censers, and put incense in them before the Lord. The three ringleaders were then separated, and the Lord caused the ground to open beneath them so that they went down live into the pit. This is the only instance in scripture of such a thing happening.

Judgement

That was not the end of the matter, however, for fire came out from the Lord, and consumed two hundred and fifty men that offered incense. In a later note we are told the judgement that fell on the two hundred and fifty became a sign, that is, it became a warning in Israel. (See Num.26:10.) And it should be a warning to us as well. "For our God is a consuming fire" (Hebs.12:29). The swift and sudden judgement that fell upon the rebels should remind us that we cannot play fast and loose with the things of God.

Nor should we be tempted to dismiss the incident of Korah's judgement lightly, arguing perhaps that it belonged to the Old Testament period. The character of God remains unchanged, and His holiness is just the same today. It was to a New Testament church Paul wrote these words, "For this cause many are weak and sickly among you, and many sleep" (1Cor.11:30). Reverence and godly fear should mark our every approach to the living God. In a day when it seems that nothing is sacred, we are in grave danger of becoming too familiar in our approachs to the living God.

Mercy

Before leaving the rebellion of Korah there is one other thing we should consider. The government of God was heavily upon that whole scene. But even then, in that overcast sky the bright rays of divine grace also shone through. This is what we read, "Notwithstanding the children of Korah died not" (Num.26:11). Clearly, the children were spared the awful judgement of their father.

The grace of God was further seen in that the children of Korah, in due course, became doorkeepers in the house of the Lord. In fact, they even became worship leaders in the service of the sanctuary. And such was their prominence in this role, two sets of psalms are actually dedicated to them. (See Psalms 42-49 & 84-88.) This must be a singular instance of the operation of God's wonderful grace. It is certainly a marvellous illustration of the scripture which says, "Where sin abounded, grace did much more abound" (Rom.5:20).

Aaron's Rod

With some justification we might have assumed that the judgement of Korah and his people would have ended the murmuring. But this was not the case. On the very next day "all the congregation of the children of Israel murmured against Moses and against Aaron, saying, You have killed the people of the Lord" (Num.16:41). This brought an immediate divine response. And in the following chapter we read how the Lord moved to vindicate Aaron as He had already vindicated Moses.

He said, "It shall come to pass that the man's rod, whom I shall choose, shall blossom" (Num.17:5). The background to this statement is full of interest. Twelve rods, each one representing the head of a tribe, were laid up overnight before the Lord. Among the rods was one for Aaron. In the morning when the rods were examined, they were found to be as they had been the night before, with one exception. The exception was Aaron's rod. There was life in Aaron's rod. "Behold, the rod of Aaron for the house of Levi was budded, and brought forth buds, and bloomed blossoms, and yielded almonds" (Num.17:8).

The budding of Aaron's rod was, beyond all doubt, the result of a direct working of divine power. It was intended to teach the people that the authority vested in Aaron was given to him from above. And it was intended to serve a further purpose as well. The Lord said, "I will make to cease from me the murmurings of the children of Israel, whereby they murmur against you" (Num.17:5). True, there were subsequent murmurings, nevertheless it would appear that they were of a different order, for after the death of Korah and his company, and the budding of Aaron's rod, the authority of Moses and Aaron was never again questioned.

The Risen Christ

In all this we should not overlook a foreshadowing of how God vindicated His Son. The life in Aaron's rod was significant indeed. The budding of that particular rod is a wonderful pointer to the resurrection of the Lord Jesus Christ. The scriptures insist that He was "declared [demonstrated] to be the Son of God with power ... by the resurrection from the dead" (Rom.1:4). The risen Lord Jesus was able to announce, "All power [authority] is given unto me in heaven and in earth" (Matt.28:18). Consequently, when the gospel of Christ was first preached to a Gentile congregation, the apostle Peter proclaimed Christ and said, "He is Lord of all" (Acts 10:36).

The Red Heifer

At this point the ordinance of the red heifer was introduced. "The Lord spoke unto Moses and unto Aaron, saying ... Speak unto the children of Israel, that they bring thee a red heifer without spot, wherein is no blemish, and upon which never came yoke ... " (Num.19:1,2). When the heifer was slain its blood was sprinkled seven times before the tabernacle, and then its body was burned without the camp.

The body was reduced to ashes which were then placed in water. This water was known in Israel as a water of purification. If someone had been excluded from the fellowship because of uncleanness, he could go and wash in that water and be cleansed from his defilement. Afterwards, when pronounced ceremonially clean, he could be received back into the fellowship of the congregation.

Believers Cleansing

All this has its New Testament counterpart in God's provision for the cleansing of believers who may have sinned. It is illustrated in the Lord's washing of the disciples feet in the upper room. (See John 13.) Paul called it "the washing of water by the word" (Eph.5:26).

The truth is plainly stated by the apostle John. He wrote, "If we confess our sins, He is faithful and just to forgive us our sins, and to cleanse us from all unrighteousness" (1John1:9). Confession is the single condition of forgiveness for believers who have sinned. When true confession is made it will always be accompanied by repentance, by a turning away from our sin, and by a plea for the Lord's forgiveness.

Many other sacrifices have to do with the guilt of sin, but the red heifer, like the trespass offering, is concerned with its defilement. Only God can forgive sin and remove its defiling stain, and the cross is the righteous basis that enables Him to do this. The sacrifice of the red heifer, therefore, speaks to us of the cross as the ground of our cleansing from defilement. Israel was a people in covenant relationship with the Holy One. They had sinned and He could not lightly pass over their sin; hence the provision of the red heifer sacrifice.

Chapter 15
Back to Kadesh

Remember, from where you are fallen,
and repent. Rev. 2:5.

At the end of the thirty-eight years of wandering, God brought the
people back to the place where the breach had occurred. He brought
them back to Kadesh Barnea. In reading the account, the first thing
that strikes us is that death was written all over that place. We
could be excused for thinking that Paul had Kadesh in mind when
he wrote to the Christians at Rome, "To be carnally minded is
death" (Rom.8:6). Immediately upon their arrival, we are told, "and
Miriam died there, and was buried there" (Num.20:1). But that is
not all, for Kadesh saw the sentence of death fall on the other leaders
as well.

Speak to the Rock

Finding no water at Kadesh, we read that the people strove again
with Moses. They said, "Why have you brought us into this evil
place? It is no place of seed, or of figs, or of vines, or of
pomegranates; neither is there any water to drink" (Num.20:5). In
due course they would come to such a place, but the time for these
things was not yet. They must be patient and wait upon God.

Moses, in characteristic fashion called upon the Lord and he was
not disappointed. For Moses was shown a rock and instructed to
"take the rod, and gather the assembly together, you, and Aaron
your brother, and speak to the rock before their eyes; and it shall
give forth its water" (Num.20:8). Alas, in an outburst of quite
understandable fustration, Moses smote the rock instead of speaking

to it, and he smote it not once but twice.

In acting as he did Moses spoiled a very wonderful type. The rock had been smitten once in the valley of Rephidim. (See Ex.17:6.) That event pointed forward to "Christ [who] was once offered to bear the sins of many" (Hebs.9:28). And now it was simply a matter of speaking to the rock, and from it would come water to slake their thirst. The instruction to speak to the rock calls to our minds what the Lord Jesus said, "how much more shall your heavenly Father give the Holy Spirit to them that ask him" (Luke 11:13).

Although the murmuring of the people was grievous in the ears of the Lord, no word of recrimination or rebuke was heard in the divine response. But what did Moses say? He stood before the rock and said, "Hear now, ye rebels; must we fetch water out of this rock? And Moses lifted up his hand, and with his rod he smote the rock twice; and the water came out abundantly, and the congregation drank, and their beasts also" (Num.20:10,11).

Moses very soon regretted what he had done, and especially what he had said. However much he may have intended otherwise, his words conveyed the impression that he was performing this miracle by his own power. Of course, his manner of speaking was perfectly natural, but therein lay its fault. This failure became the reason for Moses being barred from entering the land of promise.

Commenting on this incident the Psalmist called specific attention to what Moses said, "He spoke unadvisedly with his lips" (Psa.106:33). What Moses said was probably true, but it was not to the glory of God for him to say it. The divine displeasure was expressed in these words. "Because you believed me not, to sanctify me in the eyes of the children of Israel, therefore you shall not bring this congregation into the land which I have given them" (Num.20:12).

Moses to die in the Wilderness

This judgement became a source of very great sorrow to Moses. He besought the Lord no less than three times that the ban might be lifted. But the matter was irrevocable and non negotiable, and the Lord forbade Moses to address Him again on the subject. On the face of it, the punishment might seem to be far greater than the offence. But Moses was the law giver, and the law required obedience, especially from Moses. And since he was also the mediator of the covenant he was charged with the grave responsibility of faithfully representing God to His people.

In addition to the personal trauma of it all, the judgement should probably remind us of the scripture which says, "The law made nothing perfect, but the bringing in of a better hope did, by which we draw near to God" (Hebs.7:19). From a typical standpoint, Moses, the great lawgiver, must in the end give way to Christ. When Joshua finally superseded Moses, we probably have a further witness to the superiority of Christ.

Miriam died at Kadesh, and although Moses death did not take place until some time later, he was living on borrowed time after the return to Kadesh. (See Deut.34:5-8.) The failure of Moses on this rather sad occasion is a solemn warning to us all, and especially to those who have responsibilities of leadership among God's people. What we do and say, must be to the glory of God. And more than that, the very manner of our acting, must also minister to His glory. Our rule in all things must be, "Whether, you eat, or drink, or whatever you do, do all to the glory of God" (1Cor.10:31).

The Death of Aaron

And the same judgement fell upon Aaron. "Aaron shall be gathered unto his people; for he shall not enter into the land which I have given unto the children of Israel, because you rebelled against my word at the water of Meribah" (Num.20:24). On mount Hor, Aaron was stripped of his priestly garments, and these were put on Eleazar his son. "And Aaron died there in the top of the mount." Aaron's death again illustrates how God removes His workmen and carries on His work. For although Aaron died, the priesthood did not die with him, it continued through his successors to the blessing of their people. So we read, "and Moses and Eleazar [Aaron's son] came down from the mount" (Num.20:28).

Besides being a watershed for the children of Israel Kadesh established a principle we have proved many times. It is easier to get away in heart from the Lord, as they did, than it is to get back again. Nevertheless it is imperative that we do so. When one of the sons of the prophets cried to Elisha that he had lost the axe head in the water, the prophet asked, "Where did it fall?" And when he pointed to the spot where he lost it, the axe head was caused to swim, and that young man was then able to resume the service in which he had been engaged. (See 2Kings 6:1-7.) And for our part, the way back always begins at the point of departure.

Sometimes when individual believers, or even a church, or perhaps a group of churches, find that spiritual life is weak and the lamp is burning dim, they will ask what they must do? Their service has become so formal and mechanical, quite clearly the glory is departed and Ichabod can be written over the whole. The temptation will be to introduce human and worldly expedients but, in the end, such things will only compound their problems. They should remember instead the principal lesson of Kadesh Barnea, that the way forward is usually the way back. It has ever been true that our relations with the Lord can only be restored, when we get back to the point where they were first disordered.

Chapter 16

A New Beginning

I will be as the dew unto Israel.
Hosea 14:5.

The return to Kadesh effectively brought to an end the years of wandering. It meant that the pilgrimage proper could now be resumed. Very soon the people put Kadesh behind them and headed towards Baal-peor. This short period was a kind of parenthesis, during which the remnants of the generation that came out of Egypt finally passed from the scene, and the second generation came increasingly to the fore.

From Victory to Victory

Leaving Kadesh the children of Israel went on their conquering way. God gave them decisive victories over three notable kings. The first was a Canaanite king called Arad. The name 'Canaan' means a Merchant or a Trader. This king, therefore, seems to stand for the acquisition of material posessions, and our observation tells us that many of God's people today have allowed themselves to be taken prisoner by this particular king.

They also gained victories over two Amorite kings. The Amorites were also Canaanites, who dwelt in the mountains. The people of Israel quite decisively overcame the hostility of Sihon, king of Heshbon, and of Og, king of Bashan. Spiritually, the opposition of these two kings seems to represent the flesh, in the different ways it will oppose what is of the Lord.

These victories were really the beginning of the campaign of conquest. At this point in the journey, therefore, the people may be viewed once again as overcomers. It may be that the victory over Arad, and the two Amorite kings, together with what happened next in their encounter with Balaam, presents us with a comprehensive view of our spiritual warfare. For our foes are also three in number, they are (i) the world [Arad], (ii) the flesh [Sihon and Og] and (iii) the Devil [Balaam].

Discouragement

But this part of the journey had its down sides too. Just prior to the defeat of the two Amorite kings there was a little piece of history which has much to teach us. From mount Hor they journeyed to compass the land of Edom, which lay south of the Dead Sea. Edom is sometimes called Seir, and is referred to many times by the prophets because of its persistent antagonism to Israel. (See Ezk.35.5.)

On this occasion Moses appealed to the Edomites to allow him to pass through their territory but permission was refused. He might have retaliated, but the Lord had forbidden him saying, "Meddle not with them" (Deut.2:5). However, God did not forget Edom. And today, any visitor to Petra can see in its ruins the fulfilment of Obadiah's prophecy, who is rightly called the prophet of Edom's doom.

At this time "the soul of the people was much discouraged because of the way" (Num.21:4). And true to form, the pilgrim people once more followed their instinct and complained. For the second time they went so far as to despise the manna. This led to a severe chastening from the Lord. "The Lord sent fiery serpents among the people, and they bit the people; and many people of Israel died" (Num.21:6).

Chastisement

"Now no chastening for the present seems to be joyous, but greivous; nevertheless, afterwards it yields the peaceable fruit of righteousness unto them who are exerised by it" (Hebs.12:11). And this fiery chastisement had that precise and beneficial effect on the people. It brought home to them a true awareness of their sin. Hence we read, "Therefore the people came to Moses, and said, We have sinned; for we have spoken against the Lord, and against you" (Num.21:7).

This was only the second time in the entire journey that the people said, We have sinned. The first time followed their refusal to go up and possess the land. Afterwards they said, We have sinned, but on that occasion they did not mean it. Had they really meant it, they would have turned from their rebellious ways. But on this occasion they did mean it, for after this there was little, if any, murmuring against the Lord or against Moses. When they asked Moses to pray for them, that the Lord might remove the serpents and heal them, it was a sincere request.

The Serpent of Brass

The Lord's response was in perfect accord with His own gracious character, and it brought deliverance within the reach of all. "The Lord said unto Moses, Make a fiery serpent, and put it on a pole; and it shall come to pass, that every one that is bitten, when he looks upon it, shall live" (Num.21:8). Moses did exactly as he was instructed, and whoever was bitten and then looked was healed. The whole story is a very beautiful gospel illustration, it is actually used as such by the fourth evangelist. (See John 3:14,15.)

But what did it mean to Israel at the time? The people had sinned against the Lord in that they had rebelled against His government. This ordinance traced the evil that was in their hearts back to its source in that old serpent, the Devil. At the same time these rebellious people were brought to acknowledge their sin and to repent of it. True, the uplifted serpent, while it wonderfully typified the uplifted Jesus, did not have any virtue in itself. But by obeying the command to look, (and could anything have been more simple) the people were submitting themselves afresh to that government against which they had rebelled.

We might want to read back into this incident all the subtleties of the New Testament revelation. But this calls for caution. The issue at the time was the matter of the Lord's authority. The question was one of submission to the government of God. The people had pledged their allegiance to it, but they had rebelled against it, and now they needed to repent.

Repentance

But what does it mean to repent? True repentance is much more than a nominal expression of sorrow. It will involve a humbling of ourselves, and a turning away from our sin. Many people have deep regret, and even remorse, but this is not repentance. Sometimes their sorrow is occasioned by the fact that they have been found out, rather than because of their sin.

Real repentance will always entail a crucial change of mind, a fundamental transformation in our thinking. The first mark of truly repentant people is that they will come to think of things, not from a selfish point of view or even from the point of view of others, but from God's standpoint. Such a change will then lead on to a comprehensive commitment to the government of God, and to His glory.

The Springing Well

Israel's relationship with the Lord having been restored, the people continued their journey. They crossed the river Arnon and pressed on still until they came to a place called Beer. At Beer there was a well of water, but evidently it had become choked, and the Lord told Moses, "Gather the people together and I will give them water." We read that, "The princes digged the well, the nobles of the people digged it, by the direction of the lawgiver, with their staves." It was such a happy occasion that the congregation burst forth into spontaneous song. "Then Israel sung this song, Spring up, O well; sing ye unto it." (See Num.21:10-20.) The last time we heard the people singing like this was at the Red Sea.

There seems to be a link between these last two incidents, the uplifted serpent and the springing well. The former brings us to the Cross, the latter to the day of Pentecost, and the giving of the Spirit. Together these two happenings seem to emphasise again the link between the Lordship of Christ and the presence of the Spirit. This is a link we also noticed when after the manna was first given the people came to Rephidim. (See Ex.16.)

The Spirit Filled Life

At Rephidim they had been given water from the smitten rock, and now they received water from the well. In both instances the water speaks of the Holy Spirit. The former speaks of the gift of the Spirit while the latter, speaks more particularly of the Spirit-filled life. The Lord Jesus said to the woman at Sychar's well, "the water that I shall give him shall be in him a well of water springing up into everlasting life." (John 4:14)

It is interesting to note that centuries before Isaac had to dig again the various wells that had first been dug by his father Abraham. This was because the Phillistines had, in the meantime, filled them in with earth. (See Gen.26:18.) We need to keep digging, for the things of earth have a habit of crowding in, and choking the springing well of the Spirit, thus robbing us of the Spirit's fullness. Let us learn, not only from Isaac, but also from the nobles of Israel in the plains of Moab. (Num.21:18)

An Interlude
(The plains of Moab and Baal-peor)

Chapter 17

Balaam - the Person

They hired against you Balaam, the son of Beor. Deut.23:4.

While the people were encamped in the plains of Moab, Balaam, the false prophet suddenly appeared on the scene. Practically all we know about this strange character is that he was the son of Beor, a Midianite, and that he lived at Pethor, by the river [Euphrates].

The man himself is a puzzle wrapped up in mystery. That he possessed the gift of prophecy, and that the Lord really did speak through him is quite clear. But in his encounter with Israel in the plains of Moab he used enchantments and he is also called a soothsayer. (See Joshua 13:22.) The New Testament represents him as the epitome of covetousness and apostasy.

The Sovereignty of God

It is a remarkable witness to divine sovereignty that God actually did speak through Balaam. Revelation normally came through the chosen people, to whom had been committed the oracles of God. But this was not always the case, and Balaam is a notable exception. We know that the Lord had alerted His people to such a possibility. "In the law it is written, With men of other tongues and other lips will I speak unto this people ..." (1Cor.14:21).

In His own ministry the Lord Jesus applied this principle to his hearers. He reminded them of how the grace of God had reached beyond the borders of Israel, in the days of Elijah and Elisha. In the event, they were so incensed by that simple reminder, they took Him and would have cast Him over the brow of a hill. "But He, passing through the midst of them, went His way" (Luke 4:30).

He had merely rehearsed from their own history how the widow of Zarephath was preserved in the famine: and how Naaman, the Syrian, was cleansed from his leprosy, and neither of them had belonged to the chosen race. Why then should they have become so irate? The answer is quite simple, they had the oracles of God and they wished keep them for themselves alone. But although God had chosen Israel, He was always mindful of others also.

Balaam Called

The situation politically at this time was very delicate for the Moabites. They had already succumbed to the superior power of the Amorites. And now the very people who had conquered the Amorites were encamped on Moab's borders. A military pact with some friendly power was urgently needed. But since this option was not available, Balak, the king of Moab, sent for Balaam, who lived some four hundred miles away. Balaam had a reputation as a successful practitioner in the art of divination, and Balak wanted him to come and curse Israel.

"He sent messengers, therefore, unto Balaam ... saying, there is a people come out from Egypt: behold, they cover the face of the earth, and they abide over against me. Come now therefore, I pray you, curse me this people; for they are too mighty for me: [perhaps] I shall prevail, that we may smite them, and that I may drive them out of the land: for I [know] that whom you bless is blessed, and whom you curse is cursed" (Num.22:5,6).

Wages of Unrighteousness

At first the Lord forbade Balaam, but afterwards, knowing the thoughts of Balaam's heart, He commanded him to go. Yet Balaam was forewarned that he would be permitted to speak only the word that the Lord would speak. It's not difficult to see where Balaam stood. He was a prophet whose heart was set on money. In his case the money is called the wages of unrighteousness. He knew the course he could take with honour, but the rewards promised to him by the king of Moab were just too great a temptation. Even though the angel of the Lord withstood him, and he was rebuked by the very ass on which he was riding, Balaam persisted on his covetous way.

Upon his arrival he told Balak, "I cannot go beyond the word of the Lord my God, to do less or more" (Num.22:18). Yet his supreme motive in all that he did was greed, and this led to his downfall. It is abundantly clear that Balak too, got more than he had bargained for in hiring the prophet from Pethor. After Balaam's first parable the unhappy king exclaimed, "What have you done unto me? I took you to curse my enemies, and, behold, you have blessed them altogether" (Num.23:11). After the second parable, he protested to Balaam again and said, "Neither curse them at all nor bless them at all." But Balaam was determined to earn his wages.

The sins of parents are sometimes visited on their children. And in Balak and his people we have a striking example of this very thing. Many centuries later, when Nehemiah was governor in Jerusalem, the people of Moab were still barred from the congregation of Israel. "It was found written, that the Ammonite and the Moabite should not come into the congregation of God forever. Because they met not the children of Israel with bread and with water, but hired Balaam against them, that he should curse them" (Neh.13:1,2).

Two End Time Personages

Together Balak and Balaam seem to prefigure two characters who will appear in the last days, 'the Beast and the False Prophet'. The former conspired to curse Israel in the plains of Moab. And the latter will make war against the saints of the most high, during the great tribulation period which will come to try them who dwell on the earth. (See Rev.13.)

The interesting thing is that even in that future period of great tribulation the latter will be under the ultimate control of the same

God who overruled the activities of Balak and Balaam. Truly, He does according to His will in the army of heaven and among the inhabitants of the earth. He is "the Lord [who] has prepared His throne in the heavens, and His kingdom rules over all" (Psa.103:19).

War in Heavenly Places

Spiritual warfare in heavenly places is a reality of which our generation seems to have lost sight. We read of it in the opening chapters of Job, where God depleted the hedge He had placed around His servant. This allowed Satan to touch Job in a number of very profound ways. And all the while Job was oblivious of the fierce battle that was raging between God and Satan in the unseen realms.

Another example of this spiritual warfare in found in the book of Daniel. After three full weeks of prayer and fasting, a messenger came from the Lord to Daniel, bringing the answer to his prayers. He explained the reason for the delay; "the prince of the kingdom of Persia withstood me one and twenty days; but, lo, Michael, one of the chief princes, came to help me" (Dan.10:13). Daniel, of course, was quite unaware of these things as he waited before the Lord during that period.

And these are just sample instances of the spiritual warfare, in which Paul instructed the Ephesian believers. "For we wrestle not against flesh and blood, but against principalities, against powers, against the rulers of the darkness of this world, against spiritual wickedness in high places" (Eph.6:12). It may be that while Israel was encamped in the plains of Moab, we have a further instance of this same thing, or at least an illustration of it. In any case, it would seem, that the people were ignorant of what was happening on the hill above them.

Chapter 18

Balaam - the Parables (i)

I cannot go beyond the word of the Lord.
Num. 22:18.

Balaam came to the king of Moab intending to curse Israel, but while the words were still in his mouth, God turned them into words of the most extraordinary blessing. He asked, "How can I curse whom God has not cursed? Or how shall I defy whom the Lord has not defied?" The insert in Moses' diary for that remarkable day reads like this, "The Lord thy God would not hearken unto Balaam; but the Lord thy God turned the curse into a blessing unto thee, because the Lord thy God loved thee" (Deut.23:5).

Kingdom Prophecies

The four parables of Balaam are really four prophecies. They may have some reference to Israel in the past, perhaps to the theocratic kingdom of David and Solomon, but they relate principally to Israel in the last days. The parables link the covenant promises given to Abraham, with the coming of the King, "whose dominion shall be from sea to sea, and from the river unto the ends of the earth" (Psa.72:8).

In what is now conventionally known as the Lord's prayer, the Lord Jesus taught His people to pray for the coming of the still future messianic kingdom. Among other things they were to say, "Thy kingdom come, thy will be done in earth, as it is in heaven" (Matt 6:10). Balaam's parables anticipate the establishment of that future kingdom and the blessings that will attend Messiah's reign.

The first direct reference to such a kingdom is found in the covenant made at Sinai. The Lord said, "You shall be unto me a kingdom of priests, and an holy nation" (Ex.19:6). These words were spoken to an actual, literal, and physical people, who were encamped in the foothills of an actual, literal, and physical mountain. We must guard against the tendency, quite common today, to spiritualize the kingdom, to confuse it with the Church, or to make it something different from what it is according to scripture.

The messianic kingdom, when it is established, will have Jerusalem as its capital city, for "out of Zion shall go forth the law, and the word of the Lord from Jerusalem" (Isa.2:3). Israel's present dispersion will then be at an end. And in that day, the chosen nation, restored to the Lord and regathered to the land, will take her divinely appointed place at the head of the nations. Balaam's parables become very meaningful indeed when they are read with these things in mind.

The First Parable (Num. 23: 8-10.)

"How shall I curse whom God has not cursed? Or how shall I defy whom the Lord has not defied? For from the top of the rocks I see him, and from the hills I behold him: lo, the people shall dwell alone, and shall not be numbered among the nations. Who can count the dust of Jacob, and the number of the fourth part of Israel? Let me die the death of the righteous, and let my last end be like his!"

From the top of the rocks

Significantly, Balaam's first view of the people was from the top of a mountain. He saw them from a heavenly perspective; we might say he looked at them from God's standpoint. Israel's waywardness in the wilderness is well chronicled, and time and again, they came under the chastening hand of God. But they were still God's people, whom He had redeemed, and so far as the heathen were concerned, He saw no imperfection in them.

The difference between standing and state should always be kept in mind. Believers today are sometimes referred to in terms of their standing before God. They are in Christ; and, in Him, they are already "blessed with all spiritual blessings in heavenly places" (Eph.1:3). They are even spoken of as being already glorified. (See Rom.8:30.)

At other times, however, the believers' state is highlighted; what they are in themselves. (Compare 2 Cor.12:2. with 12:20.) But the idea is that, through the operation of the Holy Spirit in their lives, their state should increasingly be made to correspond to their standing.

The people shall dwell alone

In his first parable, the prophet from Pethor declared, "Lo, the people shall dwell alone, and shall not be reckoned among the nations" (Num.23:9). From the call of Abram, Israel had been chosen to be God's own peculiar treasure. The Lord had told His people when they were still only two months out from the house of bondage, "If you will obey my voice indeed, and keep my covenant, then you shall be a peculiar treasure unto me above all people; for all the earth is mine" (Ex.19:5).

Later, and towards the end of the wilderness journey, Moses underlined this uniquely Jewish factor. He said, "When the Most High divided to the nations their inheritance ... He set the bounds of the people according to the number of the children of Israel. For the Lord's portion is His people; Jacob is the lot of His inheritance" (Deut. 32:8,9). For this reason the seed of Abraham have always been a race apart.

It has to be significant that during the present diaspora, which has now extended to around two thousand years, although scattered among all the nations of the earth, the seed of Abraham have not been assimilated by any of them. This does not mean that Israel was meant to stand aloof, enjoying God's blessing alone, and maintaining an attitude of indifference to the nations around her.

On the contrary, Israel was uniquely intended to be the focus of God's government throughout the entire earth.

It may even be that in Balaam's first parable we are given an insight into Israel's foreign policy in the future kingdom. Restored Israel will relate peacefully to all the nations, but she will not be dependent on any of them. In those days the words of Moses will have their fulfilment. "And you shall lend unto many nations, but you shall not borrow; and you shall reign over many nations but they shall not reign over you" (Deut.15:6).

A witness against idolatry

Having said that, we should not overlook the fact that God's choice of Israel was moral as well as political. Two quite specific ideals lay behind the divine choice. In the first place, Israel was to be a witness to the nations against the evils of idolatry. Since Satan is the prime mover behind all forms of idolatry, it follows that idolatry is an abomination in God's sight.

When the God of glory appeared to him in Mesopotamia, Abraham was in all probability an idolator. But he was called away from the worship of his idols to become the father of the Hebrew race. Later, when the law was given, the worship of any god save Jehovah was emphatically ruled out. The first commandment said, "You shall have no other gods before me" (Deut.5:7). The second commandment was even more specific. This requirement was also a recurring theme and a primary emphasis in the ministry of the prophets. For instance, Isaiah reminded his hearers, "You are my witnesses, saith the Lord, that I am God" (Isa.43:12).

A people whose God is the Lord

The second ideal was that Israel should be a pattern to the nations, showing them that the secret of true happiness and prosperity, lay in a right relationship with Jehovah. We have indicated already that the best point at which to ascribe nationhood to Israel was at Sinai, for it was there the law was given.

At that time the Lord said to His people, "If you will indeed obey His voice and do all that I speak; then I will be an enemy unto your enemies, and an adversary unto your adversaries" (Ex.23:22). Such a state of affairs would undoubtedly have made Israel a profound witness among the nations of the earth. The truly marvellous thing is that these lofty ideals will yet be realised in the messianic nation in the last days.

Chapter 19

Balaam - the Parables (ii)

The Lord met Balaam and put a word in his mouth. Num. 23:16.

The Second Parable
(Num. 23: 20-24.)

"Behold, I have received commandment to bless: and He has blessed; and I cannot reverse it. He has not beheld iniquity in Jacob, neither has He seen perverseness in Israel: the Lord, his God, is with him, and the shout of a king is among them. God brought them out of Egypt; He has, as it were, the strength of [a wild ox] ..."

God is not a man, that He should repent

Balaam's pulpit had changed, and now he viewed the people from a wholly different perspective, but God had not changed, and His purpose remained the same. The Lord had already blessed this people and nothing that Balaam might say or do could alter that fact. "God is not a man, that He should lie; neither the son of man, that He should repent [change His mind]" (Num.23:19). In the face of such immutability Balaam could only cry out, "Behold, I have received commandment to bless: and He has blessed; and I cannot reverse it."

Balaam's second parable, therefore, has its focus on the blessed assurance that will mark the messianic nation in the day of the Lord's return. Although the faithfulness of God is a major theme of scripture, the truth itself comes down to a single, very simple issue. It is this: God has committed Himself in His word, and He will prove Himself true to that word. As His people, we are the recipients of exceeding great and precious promises, and these promises are reliable simply because God is faithful, He is true to His word.

Standing on the promises that cannot fail,
When the howling storms of doubt and fear assail,
By the living word of God we shall prevail,
Standing on the promises of God.

Promises to Israel and to the Church

Some people will insist on spiritualizing the promises that were given to Israel. They even go further and apportion those promises to the Church, leaving Israel to pick up the curses. To put it mildly, this is a rather cavalier way of handling the precious word. There are certain blessings promised to the Church: spiritual blessings in heavenly places in Christ. (See Eph.1:3.) There are also certain blessings pledged to Israel. And we must carefully distinguish between them. The latter are enshrined in the covenant God made with Abraham, and they relate mainly to the earth, and to the land of promise.

God promised to Abraham a seed; a literal, physical seed, a seed that would come forth out of his own loins. (See Gen.15:4.) In addition, we are told that in the same day the Lord made a covenant with Abraham saying, "Unto your seed have I given this land, from the river of Egypt unto the great river, the river Euphrates" (Gen.15:18). Can anyone doubt that this was a physical seed, or that the land was a physical land with clearly defined geographical boundaries? To make this land mean heaven would be to make a nonsense of the text. Apart from anything else, this land was preoccupied by the Kadmonites and the Girgashites etc. Pray, how did that lot come to be in heaven?

Israel restored and regathered

The promises are legion that affirm God's purpose to bring the seed of Abraham, now dispersed, back to Himself, and to regather them to the land of promise. In those days the ancient pledge of Israel's covenant-keeping God will be redeemed: "I will make of you a great nation, and I will bless you, and make your name great; and you shall be a blessing. And I will bless them that bless you, and curse him that curses you; and in you shall all families of the earth be blessed" (Gen.12:2,3). When these things come to pass all will see the ultimate proof of the faithfulness of our immutable God.

Balaam, in his second and third parables, tells of God's faithfulness in bringing His people out of Egypt. But in that coming day His faithfulness will be rehearsed in terms of how He will have brought the remnant of Israel from the four corners of the earth, and re-established them in the promised land. "Therefore, behold, the days come, saith the Lord, that it shall no more be said, The Lord liveth, who brought up the children of Israel out of the land of Egypt, but, the Lord liveth, who brought up the children of Israel from the land of the north, and from all the lands where He had driven them; and I will bring them again into their land that I gave to their fathers" (Jer.16:14,15).

Grace Abounding

This will be accomplished on the basis of Israel's national repentance, and not on the basis of her own fidelity, the lack of which was so often and so painfully displayed in the wilderness. God will again act in sovereign grace and on the ground of the atonement accomplished on Calvary's cross. For it was at Calvary that "a fountain [was] opened to the house of David and to the inhabitants of Jerusalem for sin and for uncleanness" (Zech.13:1).

It is noticeable that in all Balaam's parables the people are spoken of in terms of Jacob and Israel, and always in that order. The God of Jacob is the God who met Jacob when he had nothing and gave him everything. This speaks of God acting in sovereign grace without regard to human merit. We also know that this working of grace in Israel, in the last days, will be accompanied by a great effusion of the Spirit, thus giving the whole undertaking a tremendous spiritual dimension.

Joel prophesied of those coming days, and said, "I will pour out my Spirit upon all flesh; and your sons and your daughters shall prophesy, your old men shall dream dreams, your young men shall see visions; and, also, upon the servants and upon the handmaids in those days will I pour out my Spirit" (Joel 2:28,29). The same sort of thing actually took place at Pentecost, but quite clearly what happened then did not exhaust the meaning of this scripture.

Zechariah referred to this same spiritual dimension when he said, "And I will pour upon the house of David, and upon the inhabitants of Jerusalem, the Spirit of grace and of supplications; and they shall look upon me whom they have pierced, and they shall mourn for him, as one mourns for his only son, and shall be in bitterness for him, as one that is in bitterness for his firstborn" (Zech.12:10). Israel's present blindness will then be removed and national Israel will see that the work of the cross, accomplished so long before, is still the ground on which she can become right with God.

He has not beheld iniquity in Jacob

The cross is also the ground on which God will declare His elect a justified people. Balaam's parable anticipated this as well, he said, "He has not beheld iniquity in Jacob, neither hath He seen perverseness in Israel: the Lord, his God, is with him, and the shout of a king is among them" (Num.23:21).

An almost identical parallel to this is found in the ministry of Zephaniah. "In that day it shall be said to Jerusalem, Fear thou not; and to Zion, Let not thine hands be slack. The Lord, thy God, in the midst of thee is mighty; he will save, he will rejoice over thee with joy; he will rest in his love, he will joy over thee with singing" (Zeph.3:16,17).

After stating the foundational truth of Israel's future repentance, the prophet Isaiah went on to announce the Lord's return in these words, "the Redeemer shall come to Zion, and unto those who turn from transgression in Jacob" (Isa.59:20). He then predicted the blessing that would follow in Messiah's train. "Arise, shine; for thy light is come, and the glory of the Lord is risen upon thee. For, behold, the darkness shall cover the earth, and gross darkness the people, but the Lord shall rise upon thee, and His glory shall be seen upon thee. And the nations shall come to thy light, and kings to the brightness of thy rising" (Isa.60:1-3). Balaam put it all very succinctly, he said, "The Lord, his God, is with him, and the shout of a king is among them" (Num.23:21).

Chapter 20

Balaam - The Parables (iii)

Balaam lifted up his eyes, and he saw Israel abiding
in their tents. Num. 24: 2.

The Third Parable
(Num. 24: 5-7.)

"How goodly are your tents, O Jacob, and your tabernacles, O
Israel! Like the valleys are they spread forth, like gardens by the
river's side, like the trees of aloes which the Lord has planted, and
like cedar trees beside the waters. He shall pour water out of his
buckets, and his seed shall be in many waters, and his king shall
be higher than Agag, and his kingdom shall be exalted ..."

How goodly are your tents, O Jacob

From the top of Peor, and overlooking Jeshimon and the desert,
Balaam, in his third parable, once more contemplated Israel's
blessing in the last days. Casting his eye over the vast encampment
that spread out beneath him, he took up his parable. "How goodly
are your tents, O Jacob, and your tabernacles, O Israel! Like the
valleys are they spread forth, like gardens by the river's side, like
the trees of aloes which the Lord has planted, and like cedar trees
beside the waters" (Num.24:5,6).

Balaam was speaking, no doubt in pictorial language, of the
magnificent scene that transfixed his gaze. The whole camp had
the appearance of a garden city with beautiful tree lined avenues,
and attractive water features that extended along the entire valley.
His speech was really a parabolic portrayal of idyllic conditions
such as will only be found in the future millennial period.

We know that there was an eager anticipation of such things at the end of the wilderness wanderings. In his parting words to his people Moses said, "Happy are you, O Israel! Who is like unto you, O people saved by the Lord, the shield of your help, and who is the sword of your excellency? And your enemies shall be found liars unto you, and you shall tread upon their high places" (Deut.33:29).

But the nearest Israel ever attained to this level of blessing was in the heady days of David and Solomon. When he heard the terms of what we now call the Davidic covenant, David came and sat before the Lord. It was then he said, "What one nation in the earth is like your people, Israel, whom God went to redeem to be His own people ... for your people Israel, did you make your own people forever; and you, Lord, became their God" (1 Chron.17:21,22).

The Millennial Kingdom

Balaam's mention of the king and the kingdom is especially interesting. "His king shall be higher than Agag, and his kingdom shall be exalted" (Num.24:7). Agag was a title given to the Amalekite kings, just as the kings of Egypt were called Pharaoh, and in more recent times the ruler of Russia was known as the Czar. Since the Amalekite kingdom was, at that time, Israel's strongest foe; the reference here may be to Israel's ultimate supremacy over all the nations.

This reference to the king and the kingdom evidently looks beyond David and Solomon, to the restoration of the Davidic dynasty in the last days. This restoration was predicted by the prophet Amos, and later affirmed by the apostle James. "After this I will return, and will build again the tabernacle of David, which is fallen down; and I will build again its ruins, and I will set it up." (See Amos 9:11,12. & Acts 15:16.)

Israel's King

Israel's king in millennial times will be the Lord Jesus Christ. The angel Gabriel, in his message to the virgin mother spelt this out clearly enough. "He shall be great, and shall be called the Son of the Highest; and the Lord God shall give unto Him the throne of His father, David. And He shall reign over the house of Jacob forever; and of His kingdom there shall be no end" (Luke1:32,33). The terms used here, forever and no end, simply indicate that the millennial kingdom will flow out into the eternal state, and so, "The Lord shall reign forever and ever" (Ex.15:18).

Jeremiah, who ministered both before and during the Babylonian exile, predicted this still future restoration of the nation and of the monarchy. "Behold, the days come, saith the Lord, that I will raise unto David a righteous Branch, and a king shall reign and prosper, and shall execute justice and righteousness in the earth. In his days Judah shall be saved, and Israel shall dwell safely; and this is his name whereby he shall be called, The Lord our righteousness" (Jer.23:5,6).

What Balaam said in his third parable, therefore, clearly anticipates the time of Israel's future glory. It is a prophetic and graphic portrayal of the chosen people in the last days. To this vision we could add the combined and extended testimony of the Hebrew prophets. Although they came much later in Israel's history, they consistently, and without exception, envisaged the nation's future glory. They spoke of it as something without parallel, even in Israel's own illustrious history.

He shall pour water out of his buckets

But the blessings bestowed upon Israel in the millennial period will not be for the nation in a selfish sense. In that day, the messianic nation will become a channel of God's blessing to all the nations of the earth.

The original promise to Abraham contained this idea. "I will make of thee a great nation, and I will bless thee, and make thy name great; and thou shalt be a blessing" (Gen.12:2). And this seems to have come within the range of Balaam's vision as well, for he added, "He shall pour the water out of his buckets, and his seed shall be in many waters" (Num.24:7).

Chapter 21

Balaam - The Parables (iv)

Balaam ... said ... who saw the vision of the Almighty.

Num. 24:16.

The Fourth Parable
(Num. 24: 17-19.)

"I shall see Him, but not now: I shall behold Him, but not nigh
[near]: there shall come a star out of Jacob, and a scepter shall rise
out of Israel, and shall smite the corners of Moab, and destroy all
the children of Sheth ... Out of Jacob shall He come who shall
have dominion, and shall destroy him that remaineth of the city ..."

I shall see him, but not now.

The fourth parable propels our minds forward once more to the
day when the Lord Jesus shall be revealed in power and great glory.
Balaam said, "I shall see him, but not now; I shall behold him but
not nigh; there shall come a Star out of Jacob, and a Sceptre shall
rise out of Israel ... Out of Jacob shall he come who shall have
dominion" (Num.24:17-19). Balaam clearly foresaw the coming
of a mighty deliverer, but he could see as well that His coming
would not be immediate. Balaam was speaking of future events.

The reference to a star coming out of Jacob might call to mind the
guiding star that brought the wise men from the east at the time of
Messiah's birth. When they arrived in Jerusalem they said, "we
have seen His star in the east, and are come to worship Him"
(Matt.2:2). But Balaam's star seems to be a symbolic star, rather
than an actual light in the skies. It is not unusual in scripture for

stars or sceptres to be used as metaphors for kingly power and rule. (See Gen.49:10. & Rev.9:1.)

The Second Advent

This final parable, however, should probably be looked upon as a prophecy linking the two advents of Christ. It certainly points beyond the first, to the second, when the messianic kingdom will be established. The two advents, of course, are intrinsically connected; the first was a necessary preparation for the second. And we know that peace on earth and goodwill toward men, pledged at the first advent, will only be established at the second.

Campbell Morgan wrote, "It is impossible to read the story of the incarnation, and to believe in it, and to follow the history of the centuries that have followed upon that incarnation, without feeling in one's deepest heart that something more is needed, that the incarnation was preparatory, and that the consummation of its meaning can only be brought about by another coming, as personal, as definite, as positive, as real in human history, as was the first." ("The Purposes of the Incarnation" by G. Campbell Morgan. p.28.)

We know that "Christ was once offered to bear the sins of many; and ... He shall appear the second time without [apart from] sin unto salvation" (Hebs.9:28). Whatever differences of interpretation there may be about the timing or even the manner of His coming, the actual coming itself is plainly affirmed in this text. These words leave no room for doubt. Moreover, this text insists that while all the circumstances of the first advent were necessary to the second; the events of the second will be quite different from those of the first.

He shall have dominion

The goal of the first advent was atonement, but the goal of the second will be dominion and administration. The Lord Jesus will return as Israel's king to establish the much prayed for messianic kingdom. His coming will fulfil the scripture which says, "Behold, a king shall reign in righteousness, and princes shall rule in justice" (Isa.32:1). Balaam's vision in this final parable, will also be finally realised, for he saw a mighty deliverer coming out of Jacob to exercise dominion over all the earth.

In the purposes of God the chosen people have been set aside and are quite literally scattered among all the nations. But this is not the end of the story. God has ordained that in the last days Israel will be physically regathered to the land of promise and spiritually restored to the Lord their God. "Then shall appear the sign of the Son of Man in heaven ... and they shall see the Son of Man coming in the clouds of heaven with power and great glory. And He shall send His angels with a great sound of a trumpet, and they shall gather together His elect from the four winds, from the one end of heaven to the other" (Matt.24:30,31).

At the same time, Balaam foretold God's judgements upon Israel's foes. "And he took up his parable, and said, Alas, who shall live when God does this?" (Num.24:23) The centre and seat of divine authority in the earth was transferred from Jerusalem to Babylon in the days of Nebuchadnezzar. This change marked the beginning of the Times of the Gentiles, a prophetic period that continues to this day and will continue its course until our Lord's second advent.

The Times of the Gentiles

This prophetic period, The Times of the Gentiles, was portrayed by Daniel, the prophet, under the figure of a great image of a man. What that image represented still stands, and will continue to stand, until Messiah returns as the smiting stone. Then the feet of the great image will be smitten and the whole will be broken to pieces. (See Dan.2:44,45.)

Before the close of his ministry Daniel was given a further insight into these things. He was told, "At that time shall Michael stand up, the great prince who stands for the children of your people; and there shall be a time of trouble, such as never was since there was a nation ... and at that time your people shall be delivered, every one that shall be found written in the book" (Dan.12:1).

That time of trouble is extensively before us in the prophetic scriptures. For example, Jeremiah testified to it in no uncertain terms. "Alas! for that day is great, so that none is like it; it is even the time of Jacob's trouble, but he shall be saved out of it" (Jer.30:7). In the end, a saved remnant of Israel will emerge from the crucible of that great tribulation period to assume the headship of the nations in our Lord's millennial kingdom. Balaam's parables need to be read in the light of those astounding 'end time' events.

Chapter 22
Balaam - The Doctrine

Balaam, taught Balak to cast a stumbling block before the
children of Israel. Rev. 2:14.

Separated, comforted and blessed, here was a people who could
not be cursed. Yet Balaam had to earn the rewards promised to
him by Balak. What could he do? There was one thing that could
be done. This people could not be cursed but they could be
corrupted!

Before he returned to the mountains of Pethor, Balaam came again
before the king of Moab and showed him how this end could be
achieved. He "taught Balak to cast a stumbling block before the
children of Israel, to eat things sacrificed unto idols, and to commit
fornication" (Rev.2:14).

Israel Compromised

What followed the worship of the golden calf in the plains of Sinai
should have been a sufficent warning to preserve the people from
what was now proposed. As a result of that earlier excursion into
similar territory, they had come under a most severe chastening
from the Lord. And when Moses interceded with God on behalf of
His people at that time, he asked, "Wherein shall it be known here
that I and your people have found grace in your sight? Is it not in
that you go with us? So shall we be separated, I and your people,
from all the people that are upon the face of the earth" (Ex.33:16).
But all that seems to have been conveniently forgotten.

From the beginning it was God's intention that Israel should keep herself free from entanglements with other nations. But she was slow to learn that her true confidence was in God and not in political alliances. At the beginning of his reign in Jerusalem, king Asa acted on this principle. "He took away the altars of the strange gods ... And commanded Judah to seek the Lord God of their fathers ... and the kingdom was quiet before him" (2Chron.14:3-5). On that basis Asa successfully defended himself against every aggressor.

Later, he foolishly set aside this principle, and instead of trusting in the Lord for his defence, he relied on military pacts. Very soon Asa found himself in all kinds of difficulties. (See 2Chron.16:7-10.) In the end, just before he died he became diseased in his feet. Could it be that his physical affliction was simply a reflection of his spiritual condition? In his last days Asa was certainly not walking as he did in his first days, when he walked in simple dependence on the Lord.

This principle of separation has an abiding application to believers in every age. Without being in any sense sectarian in our attitudes, we are called to walk in manifest separation to the Lord. "Let us go forth, therefore, unto Him without the camp, bearing His reproach" (Hebs.13:13). This means that separation is primarily a positive thing. Alas, we are about to see, in the events of Baal-peor, how Israel failed grievously at this very point. And it is here that the church has so manifestly failed as well. The church in the world is one thing, but the world in the church is something different.

Baal-peor

The religion of Moab was a worshipping of demons, in turn, this involved all kinds of attendant evils and impurities. By inviting the people of Israel to attend their religious festivals, the Moabites enticed them into idolatry and through that they seduced them into fornication. "The people began to commit [harlotry] with the daughters of Moab. And the people bowed down to their gods. And Israel joined himself unto Baal-peor" (Num.25:1-3).

We are told this provoked the Lord to anger and precipitated a situation that moved Him to make a final end of the generation that had come out of Egypt. Moses told the judges, "Slay every one his men that were joined to Baal-peor" (Num.25:5). But this was only the beginning. A great plague swept through the host, killing a total of twenty four thousand people.

It would seem that this terrible scene of disease and death marked the end of the generation that had turned back from entering Canaan thirty-eight years earlier. The proof of this lies in the fact that immediately after the plague had been stayed, a commandment was given to number the new generation. (See Num.26:1,2.)

Phinehas the High Priest's Son

But there was one bright spot in that dark scene. The background to it was a certain evil that had taken place.   A man of Israel brought home to his tent a woman of Midian. The evil was compounded by the fact that the man concerned was a prince of a chief house of Simeon: his name was Zimri, the son of Salu. The woman's name was Cozbi, the daughter of Zur, who was also head of a chief house of Midian. The evil was both brazen and public. It took place in the sight of Moses and the whole congregation. And it occured at the very time when the people were still in bitter remorse over their recent failure.

But a young man called Phinehas, the high priest's son, when he saw what was done, took a javelin and went into the tent and summarily dealt with them both. The brave action of Phinehas that day earned him an immediate commendation. The Lord said, "Phinehas ... has turned my wrath away from the children of Israel, while he was zealous for my sake among them ... Behold, I give unto him my covenant of peace. And he shall have it, and his seed after him, even the covenant of an everlasting priesthood, because he was zealous for his God, and made an atonement for the children of Israel" (Num.25:11-13).

That timely deed, while it brought to an end the plague that had fallen on Israel, had called for quite exceptional personal courage. For one thing, Phinehas risked exposing himself to the censure of his own people. And for this reason alone his exploit occupies a deserving mention in the history to this day. There will be times when personal and parochial considerations must be set aside for the sake of the larger testimony of God among us.

The courageous and decisive action taken by Phinehas had a threefold result. In the first place, it honoured the Lord, and for this reason God honoured him. Then it brought a very great deliverance to the people. Finally, it completely thwarted the evil purposes of Israel's enemies, and the wicked conspiracy of Balaam and of Barak.

When Joshua eventually avenged Moab's treachery, the sword of justice fell heavily on Balaam. "Balaam also, the son of Beor, the soothsayer, did the children of Israel slay with the sword ... " (Josh.13:22). Balaam and Barak had proved formidable foes, but the Lord was with Israel as He is with His people today. "What shall we then say to these things? If God be for us, who can be against us?" (Rom.8:31) The essential message is quite simple: the living God will always have the last word.

All these varied happenings brought the fourth stage of the journey to an end. The way was once again cleared for the purpose of God to be realised. The many years of wandering and of barrenness at last were at an end. The long awaited and final leg of the journey, which would bring the second generation across the Jordan and into the promised land, was about to begin.

Stage Five
Home at last
(From the plains of Moab to the Promised Land)

Chapter 23
Time to leave the wilderness

Every place that the sole of your foot shall tread upon, that have
I given unto you. Joshua 1:3.

The rest of the book of Numbers is very largely the record of the
many preparations that had to be made for the entry into Canaan.
The encampment in the plains of Moab before they crossed over
Jordan, was memorable for several reasons. Besides the events
already referred to, other momentous things were still to take place
there. But from all the matters that might elicit our interest, we
shall select just three.

(i) A Second Census

Not least among the things still pending was the command to
number the people. "Take the sum of all the congregation of the
children of Israel, from twenty years old and upward, throughout
their fathers' house, all who are able to go to war in Israel"
(Num.26:2).

The book of Numbers takes its name, of course, from the two
recorded numberings of the people. One at the beginning of the
journey and the other at its end. The first was at Sinai and is
connected with their deliverance from Egypt. (See Num.1:1-4.)
The other was here in the plains of Moab and is connected with
their entrance into Canaan.

The Remnant and the Messianic Hope

It is a poignant fact that at this second numbering only two remained, of the more than six hundred thousand men of war who were first numbered. Of the rest we are told, "They were overthrown in the wilderness" (1 Cor.10:5). The two who remained were Caleb and Joshua. Because of the promises given to them, they embodied in a living way Israel's hope of entry into the land. Moreover, their continuance represented a material link with the deliverance from Egypt. These two men were living witnesses to the continuity of God's purpose.

Discussing Israel's present dispersion and future recovery, Paul declared, "At this present time also there is a remnant according to the election of grace" (Rom.11:5). During this present interval of the church, while Israel nationally has been set aside, there always have been a number of Jews who have believed the gospel of our Lord Jesus Christ. These saved Jews share equally with believing Gentiles, in the privilege of being part of the body of Christ.

But more than that, their very existence, like a beacon, keeps alive the messianic hope: the hope that Israel, now dispersed, will finally be restored to the Lord and returned to the land. They do this in much the same way as Caleb and Joshua, during those thirty-eight years of wandering in the wilderness, kept alive the hope of entry into the land.

Who Entered the Land?

We have seen how Aaron gave way to Eleazar, and soon Moses must give way to Joshua. Here, in the plains of Moab, the generation that came out of Egypt finally gave way to a wholly new generation. Caleb and Joshua certainly entered the promised land with this new generation. But taking a larger view, it seems there were others, besides these two, who had come out of Egypt and were now to enter Canaan.

The Levites had earlier been set apart for sanctuary service, and were not therefore men of war. Levi was recognized as the priestly tribe because Levi had remained true to the Lord and to Moses, in the plains of Sinai. Moreover, since the Levites had not sent any representative to spy out the land, they were not implicated in the evil report brought back to Kadesh Barnea.

The prohibition upon entering the land, following the failure of Kadesh was placed, fairly and squarely, on all that were men of war, who came out of Egypt. (See Josh.5:6.) But for the reasons just enumerated, Levi was exempted from the statute prohibiting the men of war, save Caleb and Joshua, from entering Canaan. But even allowing for that, only a very small remnant of the original company actually entered the land.

Caleb and Joshua

We must not overlook the fact that the entry of Caleb and Joshua into Canaan was, in the first place, a reward for their faithfulness. At Kadesh, when Israel turned back, and limited the Holy One of Israel, these two remained loyal and stood strong in faith. In His anger the Lord swore, saying, "Surely none of the men who came up out of Egypt, from twenty years old and upward [ie. the men of war], shall see the land which I swore to give unto Abraham, unto Isaac, and unto Jacob, because they have not wholly followed me. Save Caleb, the son of Jephunneh, the Kenizite, and Joshua, the son of Nun; for they have wholly followed the Lord" (Num.32:11,12).

Behind the expression, wholly followed the Lord, lies the image of a shepherd and his dog. Just as the sheepdog is responsive to every signal from its master, however oblique, so Caleb and Joshua followed the Lord. At a great banquet, the trained servants who wait on the guests, will understand even the movement of the host's finger and will respond accordingly. This is evidently the kind of imagery the Psalmist had in mind when he wrote, "Behold, as the eyes of servants look unto the hand of their masters, and as the eyes of a maiden unto the hand of her mistress, so our eyes wait upon the Lord our God, until He has mercy upon us" (Psa.123:2). This verse found an apt expression in Caleb and Joshua during those years of wandering.

Caleb's Reward

We have still quite a lot to say about Joshua, but our present work will not extend to the reward Caleb received when Israel entered the land. We might simply note at this point, therefore, that when he was eighty-five years of age, he claimed his possession. Reminding Joshua of the pledge Moses had given him at Kadesh, he said, "Now therefore give me this mountain ... And Joshua blessed him, and gave to Caleb ... Hebron for an inheritance" (Joshua 14:12,13).

Caleb's inheritance was the Canaanite city of Kirjath-arba, better known to us as Hebron, and its surrounding area. It was the portion of the land Caleb had traversed almost forty years earlier when, with the others, he had come to spy out Canaan. Hebron, lies about twenty miles south of Jerusalem, and is one of the oldest cities on earth. Abraham, Isaac, and Jacob all lived there, and Sarah died there and was buried in the cave of Machpelah. For a time, David reigned in Hebron. In the days of Caleb and Joshua it became one of the six cities of refuge.

(ii) The Two and a Half Tribes

In readiness for entry to Canaan, Moses was told to prepare to lay down his task and, at the same time, to prepare Joshua to take it up. But before either of these things happened, there were other pressing matters to be settled. The two and a half tribes (the tribes of Reuben and Gad, and the half tribe of Manasseh) came to Moses demanding to have their inheritance on the wilderness, or eastern, side of Jordan. They were determined to settle in the territories taken from Sihon, king of the Amorites, and from Og, king of Bashan.

As we have seen, the children of Israel overthrew both these kings before they came to the plains of Moab. A land of fullness was set before them and it was God's will that they should possess it, but the two and a half tribes would settle for less. Significantly, they were constrained in all this by a purely materialistic motive. They said of their desired portion, "It is a land for cattle, and thy servants have cattle" (Num.32:4).

Moses saw in the request of the two and a half tribes a parallel with what their fathers had done at Kadesh, and he told them so in no uncertain terms. But although he rebuked them at first, he afterwards gave his reluctant consent. Here we seem to have a further example of a matter that has cropped up again and again. At times God seems to condescend to meet His people in the state in which He finds them.

Moses was also mindful of the possible effect their decision could have on the other tribes. He said, "Shall your brethren go to war, and shall you sit here? Why do you discourage the heart of the children of Israel from going over into the land which the Lord has given them?" (Num.32:6,7) But they declared their willingness to leave their families, and go with their brethren, and to fight for the land. The weakness of this line of action was that it would leave their wives and their children exposed, and at the mercy of marauding tribespeople. Moreover, their hearts would hardly be in the fight since they had no desire to dwell in the conquered territory.

Nor is it difficult to discern in all this, important spiritual insights for today. So often believers are content to stop short of God's revealed will for their lives and to settle for a life of carnal ease. They leave their first love, and become cold in heart. They begin to esteem lesser things, such as material possessions, of greater worth than their heritage in Christ. They no longer press on, as once they did, toward the mark for the prize of the high calling of God in Christ Jesus. As a result, they often become a source of discouragement to their brethren. Perhaps the worst consequence of all is that they expose their offspring to the allurements of this godless world, and to the wiles of the devil.

The Alternative Altar

What could not have been foreseen in the plains of Moab, was the long-term effect of this decision to break ranks. Some seven years later, and after a hard struggle, the land was subdued and the tribes were settled in their various inheritances. Imagine the alarm that was caused when it was discovered that the two and a half tribes had set up a great altar in the borders of Jordan. It probably was a replica of the altar of God at the gate of the tabernacle.

In practical terms, this rival altar was the visible sign that the unity of the people of God was now seriously breached. In the beginning of the book of Joshua, we find the people united to fight their common enemies. But at the end of the book we find them preparing to fight what amounted to internecine warfare. "And when the children of Israel heard of it, the whole congregation of Israel gathered themselves together at Shiloh, to go up to war against them [the two and a half tribes]" (Josh.22:12).

In the event Phinehas was sent, with a deputation of princes, to challenge the two and a half tribes. The delegation presented the feeling of the whole congregation in the sternest possible terms. (The whole congregation here must mean the whole congregation apart from the two and a half tribes.) The delegates likened the great altar to the iniquity of Baal-peor, and to the sin of Achan at Jericho, for which the people had suffered the righteous indignation of the Lord.

But the two and a half tribes put this very genuine concern down to a simple misunderstanding. They undertook to give the altar a name that seemed quite acceptable to the delegates. When this was agreed the deputation returned with their report, and we are told "the thing pleased the children of Israel" (Josh.22:33). Happily, and for the time being, open warfare was averted, but we cannot say that God was well pleased.

Their Later History

The later history of these tribes makes disturbing reading. After the death of Solomon, the kingdom was divided into two parts. The northern kingdom, comprising the ten northern tribes, had its capital in Samaria, and became known as Israel. In due course, a king reigned over this northern kingdom called Jehu. Of him it is stated, "But Jehu took no heed to walk in the law of the Lord God of Israel with all his heart; for he departed not from the sins of Jereboam, who made Israel to sin." At that time the Lord used Hazael, the king of Syria, to judge Israel. But only a part, the most vulnerable part, was cut off. Significantly, that part was "From the Jordan eastward, all the land of Gilead, the Gadites, and the Reubenites, and the Manassites." (See 2Kings 10:29-33.)

It may well be that the Gadarenes in our Lord's day were later descendants of the Gadites. If that is so, it is both interesting and significant that the same materialistic spirit seems to have governed them as had governed their forbears. The Lord Jesus permitted the evil spirits exorcised from the man who dwelt in the tombs, to enter into a herd of swine. The swine then ran down a steep place and were drowned in the sea. But when the Gadarenes came out from the city, they besought the Saviour to depart. This was not the first time, and it certainly was not the last, when property was prized above people. (See Luke 8:26-40.)

There were, of course, happier moments in the chequered story of the two and a half tribes. For instance, when David was in the wilderness hiding from Saul, a band of mighty men rallied to his cause. Some of those men, notably Jephthah and Barzillai, came from the tribe of Gad. They were "men of might, and men of war fit for the battle, that could handle shield and buckler, whose faces were like the faces of lions, and were as swift as the roes upon the mountains" (1Chron.12:8). Nevertheless, the tortuous course of the two and a half tribes, following their decision to settle east of Jordan, serves to warn us of the dangers of a Christian life that falls short of that good, and acceptable, and perfect will of God.

(iii) The Death of Moses

The last chapter of Deuteronomy records how Moses finally laid down his task. Faithful to Him who appointed him, Moses was also the meekest of men. To others the Lord made Himself known in visions, and He spoke to them in dreams. It was different with Moses; the Lord spoke to him face to face, and plainly, rather than in dark sayings. But the time had now come for Moses to die. He was to find an unmarked grave on a lonely hillside.

The apostle Jude referred to a dispute between the archangel Michael and the Devil, over the body of Moses. (See Jude.9.) We need not speculate on the report since no other reference is made to it in scripture. What we do know is clearly stated in the obituary. It reads: "And Moses went up from the plains of Moab unto the mountain of Nebo, to the top of Pisgah ... So Moses the servant of the Lord died there in the land of Moab" (Deut.34:1&5).

And no man knows that sepulchre,
For no man saw it ere;
T'was the angel of God, upturned the sod,
And laid the dead man there.

Earlier, we heard the false prophet from Pethor say he wanted to die the death of the righteous, but Balaam had no wish to live the life of the righteous. Here in the death of Moses we have an outstanding instance of the death of a righteous man. We are told that in the day of his death Moses went up. For the believer today, death is like that; it is a departing to be with Christ which is far better.

For Moses that was also the day when faith gave way to sight. "The Lord showed him all the land of Gilead, unto Dan, and all Napthali, and the land of Ephraim, and all the land of Judah, unto the utmost sea" (Deut.34:1&2). For forty years Moses had seen the land, but only by the eye of faith, and through a glass darkly, now he saw it as it really was. In like manner, the believer finds that in death the veil of sense is lifted and he is face to face with Christ his Saviour.

Only faintly now I see Him,
With the darkling veil between;
But a blessed day is coming,
When His glory shall be seen.

Moses was one hundred and twenty years old when he died, yet he did not die of old age. Nor did he die of ill health; for his eye was not dim, nor his natural force abated. Scripture tells us that he died according to the word of the Lord. "So Moses, the servant of the Lord, died there in the land of Moab, according to the word of the Lord" (Deut.34:5). Believers have always found great comfort in the knowledge that their times are in God's hand. The record of Moses life and death is a wonderful confirmation of that conviction.

Chapter 24

Joshua becomes Leader

As I was with Moses, so I will be with you.
Joshua 1:5.

God removes His workmen and carries on His work. He had brought Israel out of Egypt under Moses, and now He would bring them into Canaan under Joshua. And so we read, "Now after the death of Moses, the servant of the Lord, it came to pass that the Lord spoke unto Joshua, the son of Nun, Moses' minister, saying, Moses, my servant, is dead; now therefore arise, go over this Jordan, thou and all this people, unto the land which I do give to them, even to the children of Israel" (Josh.1:1,2).

The Title Deeds

Canaan had been given to Abraham by promise as part of the Abrahamic covenant. God had said, "Unto thy seed have I given this land, from the river of Egypt unto the great river, the river Euphrates" (Gen.15:18). And this covenant was later confirmed to Isaac and also to Jacob. The land was then given to Moses by redemption. We have already considered the pledges given to Moses at the burning bush, concerning the land.

And now the land promised to Abraham, and also to Moses, was to be given to Joshua by conquest. God would give them the land but it was their's to possess it. Israel's title to the land, therefore, is well established. And although presently scattered among all nations, she will possess the land in a coming day on the basis of that title. The first twelve chapters of the book of Joshua are about the conquest of Canaan, and the final twelve chapters are about its possession.

Joshua

The name Joshua was originally Oshea, or Hoshea, but Moses linked it with part of the divine name Jehovah, so that it became Jehoshua which was later shortened to Joshua. The New Testament equivalent is Jesus. The name means, in Jehovah is salvation. Since Joshua took over from Moses, not as law-giver, but as leader, he seems to be a type of Christ as the Captain of our salvation.

At the Red Sea Moses had two words for the people, (i) stand still and (ii) go forward. Now, upon his appointment, Joshua also had two words for his people. The first was, Prepare. He commanded the people to prepare for entry into the land. They were to make ready food supplies for within three days they would pass over Jordan, to possess that good land, which had long been promised to them.

Joshua's second word was like the first, Sanctify yourselves. (Josh.3:5) When the three days had passed his officers went through the host with this further message, at once important and precise. Besides preparing supplies they were to prepare themselves. The officers also instructed the people saying, "When you see the ark of the covenant of the Lord your God, and the priests the Levites bearing it, then you shall remove from your place, and go after it" (Josh.3:3).

Across Jordan

The people might have succumbed once again to the defeatism of Kadesh Barnea. They might have argued that Jericho was well fortified, and that the men of Jericho would put up a stout resistance. They might even have argued that the time was not right. After all, it was harvest time and the river was in flood. "For Jordan overflows all its banks all the time of harvest" (Josh.3:15).

But faith was strong, as it had been at the beginning, and they went forward counting upon God. In the event, as soon as the priests' feet rested in the waters of Jordan, the river divided and all the Israelites passed over on dry ground. They could have had no hesitation whatsoever in saying that the Lord was with them, for this dividing of the river, at the least propitious time, when the Jordan overflowed its banks, proclaimed that with God all things are possible. In crossing over they observed the two things that had been asked of them. They went after the ark, and they allowed about two thousand cubits to come between them and the ark (Josh.3:3,4).

Spiritual minds have always discerned in the children of Israel going after the ark (itself a marvellous type of Christ), a picture of believers following the Lord. From the beginning this is the ideal that has inspired Christian living. The Lord's first word to Simon Peter was, "Follow me, and I will make you fishers of men." Interestingly, this was His last word to Peter as well. (Compare Matt.4:19 & John 21:22.) We must never forget that we too are followers of the Lamb.

The further instruction about keeping their distance would allow every person in the host to have an uninterrupted view of the ark. Otherwise the vast majority of the people would have been like Zacchaeus of Jericho, who could not see Jesus because of the crowd. The message here seems to be that we must always maintain a clear view of Christ. For it is only by looking unto Jesus that we will be able to run with patience the race that is set before us.

Oh, pilgrim bound for the heavenly land,
Never lose sight of Jesus.
By day and by night, He will keep you right,
Never lose sight of Jesus.

The two thousand cubits may also have been a reminder to them of the holiness of God, for the ark of the covenant was the symbol of God's presence in the midst of His people. A becoming reverence was needed on their part, as it is on our part today, when we draw aside into the presence of the Lord.

Two Memorials

At that time Joshua commanded the setting up of two memorials. One was set up in the midst of Jordan where the priests had stood until the people were all passed over. "And Joshua set up twelve stones in the midst of Jordan" (Josh.4:9). The other was established in Gilgal, on the side of Jordan where their inheritance lay. "And those twelve stones, which they took out of the Jordan, did Joshua set up in Gilgal" (Josh.4:20). Both these memorials, each consisting of twelve stones, represented the people as a whole, all twelve tribes of Israel.

The two memorials, one in the Jordan and the other out of the Jordan, seem to point to the dying and the rising again of our Lord Jesus Christ. We need to go further and say that they are a typical witness to the believer's identification with Him in His death and resurrection. "If we have been planted together in the likeness of His death, we shall be also in the likeness of His resurrection" (Rom.6:5).

Instructing the Children

But the immediate purpose of the memorials should not be overlooked. They were erected as object lessons to be used in the instruction of the children. "That this may be a sign among you, that when your children ask their fathers in time to come, saying, What mean you by these stones? Then you shall answer them, That the waters of Jordan were cut off before the ark of the covenant of the Lord; when it passed over Jordan" (Josh.4:6,7).

Since, in the nature of things, children have always been inveterate questioners, Joshua knew that the memorials would excite their curiosity and lead them to ask questions. This in turn, would give parents the opportunity, without anything being forced, to tell their children of the marvellous acts of the Lord, which He wrought on behalf of His people.

But Joshua also urged the people to view these things in the broad context of the purposes of God, and to actively and objectively teach those purposes to their children. "You shall let your children know, saying, Israel came over this Jordan on dry land ... That all the people of the earth might know the hand of the Lord, that it is mighty, that you might fear the Lord your God forever" (Josh.4:20-24).

In this way the memory of these extraordinary happenings would be secured for succeeding generations. Moses seemingly had been deeply concerned about the people's proneness to forget. Repeatedly he exhorted them to remember, and to beware that they forget not. Indeed, such exhortations form the basis of the entire book of Deuteronomy. Clearly, Joshua too, had the same concern. And because we too have a tendency to forget, the Lord Jesus instituted the Christian's memorial supper and said, "This do in remembrance of me" (Luke 22:19).

Chapter 25
Canaan - the First Days

The children of Israel encamped ... in the plains of Jericho.
Joshua 5:10.

It was on the tenth day of the first month that the people crossed over Jordan. The place of their encampment was Gilgal, which lay due east of Jericho. Gilgal features a great deal in their possession of the land, and the spiritual meaning of what took place there has deep significance for us. "At that time the Lord said to Joshua, Make sharp knives, and circumcise again the children of Israel the second time" (Josh.5:2). Apparently the generation that came out of Egypt had been circumcised and now this rite was to be performed on the second generation. But what does Gilgal have to say to us today?

The Meaning of Gilgal

We have the New Testament definition of circumcision, in the epistle to the Colossians. Paul declared, "In [Christ] you are circumcised with the circumcision made without hands ... And you, being dead in your sins and the uncircumcision of your flesh, has He made alive together with Him, having forgiven you all trespasses" (Col.2:11-13). Circumcision, therefore, is a spiritual thing for believers today. It takes place, not at baptism, but at the time of our new birth: when we become In Christ and when we receive the forgiveness of sins.

In its spiritual meaning circumcision makes prominent the fact that when Christ died, His death was not only for sin, it was also to sin. "For in that He died, He died unto sin ... " (Rom.6:10). And when He died, we died in Him: His death was our death. We must not confuse this with baptism in water, for water baptism is simply an outward confession and confirmation of what has already taken place in the inward and spiritual realm.

The circumcision at Gilgal, however, while it confronts us with this truth, also insists on its practical outworking in our lives. Paul pressed this on the Colossians believers. He said: "Mortify, therefore, your members which are upon the earth: fornication, uncleanness, inordinate affection, evil [desire], and covetousness (which is idolatry)" (Col.3:5). In a word, circumcision teaches the necessity of bringing the death of Christ to bear on our members in self-discipline and self-judgement. We are usually good at judging other people, but we would be better Christians if we judged ourselves.

Back to Gilgal

The fact that the children of Israel returned to Gilgal after every battle should not be overlooked. And yet there was a single and notable exception to that rule. After the victory of Jericho, they went on to Ai, without first repairing to Gilgal. Ai was such an insignificant place they were confident they could overthrow it by their own strength. In fact, they sustained a humiliating defeat. And so sharply were they repulsed at Ai, they never again neglected Gilgal.

Reproach

Following this mass circumcising of the people, the Lord said to Joshua, "This day have I rolled away the reproach of Egypt from off you. Wherefore the name of the place is called Gilgal [meaning 'a rolling'] to this day" (Josh.5:9). There are two reproaches mentioned in scripture, the reproach of Egypt, which speaks of the world, and the reproach of Christ.

All true believers are viewed as bearing reproach. If we are not bearing the reproach of Christ in the eyes of the world, then we are bearing the reproach of the world in the eyes of the Lord. The clarion cry to us all is this, "Let us go forth, therefore, unto Him without the camp, bearing His reproach. For here we have no continuing city, but we seek one to come" (Hebs.13:13,14). This is the abiding challenge of Gilgal.

Passover in Canaan

While they were still at Gilgal the people kept the passover. The first time they had kept this feast was in Egypt. That was the original passover, and it was unique. Every other passover was a memorial of the first. There is one instance of the passover having been observed in the wilderness, and now for the first time it was observed in the land. The original passover carries us back in thought to the cross when Jesus suffered and died. But the second and subsequent passovers bring us to the communion service; sometimes referred to as the Lord's Supper, or the Breaking of Bread.

The fact that no question of moral fitness was raised at the original passover in Egypt, teaches us that when we come to the cross in repentance and faith, we come just as we are, poor sinners, lost and helpless. But at the second passover, questions of suitability were raised. (See Num.9:1-14.) To observe the Lord's Supper without first examining ourselves is a sure recipe for the whole exercise to become a matter of mere form and ceremony. The Jews had their preparation for the Sabbath and we need to have our preparation for the Lord's day.

Christian believers should never forget the apostolic appeal connected with the observance of the Lord's Supper. "Let a man examine himself, and so let him eat of this bread, and drink of this cup. For he that eats and drinks unworthily, eats and drinks [judgement] to himself, not discerning the Lord's body" (1Cor.11:28,29). The very fact that Gilgal was the place where the passover was first celebrated in the land, is a timely reminder of our need for self-judgement in coming before the Lord.

The Old Corn of the Land

Before they launched their campaign to subdue the land, a final detail is called to our notice. The day following the passover, they ate of the old corn of the land. "And the manna ceased on the next day after they had eaten of the old corn of the land; neither had the children of Israel manna any more, but they did eat of the fruit of the land of Canaan that year" (Josh.5:12).

The manna had been the wilderness food of the people. It speaks to us of the Lord Jesus in His pathway through this scene. The old corn of the land, which lay beyond Jordan, speaks of Him now risen and exalted. We feast on the old corn of the land when we dwell upon the truth of our union with the risen Lord Jesus in heavenly places. "Blessed be the God and Father of our Lord Jesus Christ, who has blessed us with all spiritual blessings in heavenly places in Christ" (Eph.1:3).

Harvest times in Israel coincided with the various feasts. First came the barley harvest at the time of Passover and First Fruits. This was also the time of Israel's entry into the land. Then, a little later, came the wheat harvest, and later still the vintage, or grape harvest. Moses had predicted that when the people entered the land, they would come to cities which they had not built, houses full of all good things, which they had not filled, wells which they had not dug, and vineyards and olive trees which they had not planted. In his final address to the nation Joshua freely acknowledged that what had been predicted had been fully realised. (See Deut.6:10,11.& Josh.24:13.)

Faithfulness of God

It had been a long and, at times, a turbulent journey. They had been on the heights, but more often they were in the hollows. They had provoked the Lord to anger, and they had sinned against themselves. Yet Joshua's closing testimony, was a forthright and unqualified affirmation of the faithfulness of God. He said, "Not one thing has failed of all the good things which the Lord your

God spoke concerning you; all are come to pass unto you, and not one thing has failed thereof" (Josh.23:14).

Moses, just before he died, had paid a similar tribute to the faithfulness of God. "Ask your father, and he will show you; your elders, and they will tell you ... the Lord's portion is his people; Jacob is the lot of His inheritance. He found him in a desert land ... he led him ... he instructed him ... he kept him as the apple of His eye" (Deut.32:7-10). The apple [pupil] is that part of the eye requiring special protection, and Moses testimony succinctly and beautifully expressed God's watchful care of His people.

At the burning bush the promise to Moses was emphatic and plain. "I am come down to deliver them ... to bring them up ... unto a large and good land, unto a land flowing with milk and honey" (Ex.3:8). That pledge had been redeemed. Moreover, the integrity of the covenant made with Abraham some four hundred years earlier had been spectacularly maintained. When we say that God is faithful, we mean that He is true to His word. And Israel's historic journey from Egypt to Canaan gives us solid grounds for believing that when we take our stand on the promises of God, we are resting on promises that will never fail.

Subject Index